Lessons for the Living

Lessons *for the* Living

Stories of Forgiveness, Gratitude, and Courage at the End of Life

STAN GOLDBERG

TRUMPETER
Boston & London
2009

The names of the people I've served have been changed and information that would compromise their families' privacy has been removed.

TRUMPETER BOOKS
An imprint of Shambhala Publications, Inc.
Horticultural Hall
300 Massachusetts Avenue
Boston, Massachusetts 02115
www.shambhala.com

9 8 7 6 5 4 3 2 1

First Edition

PRINTED IN THE UNITED STATES OF AMERICA

⊗ This edition is printed on acid-free paper that meets the American National Standards Institute z39.48 Standard.

♻ This book was printed on 30% postconsumer recycled paper.
For more information please visit us at www.shambhala.com.
Distributed in the United States by Random House, Inc., and in Canada by Random House of Canada Ltd

Designed by Steve Dyer

Library of Congress Cataloging-in-Publication Data
Goldberg, Stanley A.
Lessons for the living: stories of forgiveness, gratitude, and courage at the end of life / Stan Goldberg.—1st ed.
p. cm.
ISBN 978-1-59030-676-5 (hardcover: alk. paper)
1. Goldberg, Stanley A. 2. Hospice care—United States—Biography.
3. Prostate—Cancer—Patients—United States—Biography. I. Title.
R726.8.G646 2009
362.17'5092—dc22
[B]
2008051927

To those teachers
who by their graciousness and courage
taught me to live, no matter how long
that may be

Contents

Acknowledgments

THIS BOOK would never have been possible without the encouragement of my fellow hospice volunteers, and the dedicated efforts of those people who trained me. Thanks to the patients and families who invited me into their lives. I've done my best to protect their true identities. I thank those surviving family members who granted me permission to share their stories here. Thanks also to Wendy, Jessica, and Justin for their patience and understanding. Dr. Joseph Spaulding and Dr. George Kimmerling for their compassionate medical care. The unending efforts of Chris Morehouse of Dunham Literary. The excellent editorial advice of Elsa Dixon. The important and critical comments of the Blackhawk Writers Group and the San Francisco Writer's Group. The Zen Hospice Project, George Mark Children's House, Hospice By The Bay, Maitri, and Coming Home Hospice for providing me with opportunities to serve. To Ben Gleason for his thoughtful editorial suggestions. And finally, the support of Emily Bower of Shambhala, who allowed me to publish with a company I hold in awe.

Lessons for the Living

Introduction

> The aim of life is to live, and to live means
> to be aware, joyously, drunkenly, serenely,
> divinely aware.
>
> —Henry Miller

My life is tethered to a number few people have ever heard of—a Gleason score of 7. It's a measure of prostate cancer severity that ranges from a forgettable number 1 to a terminal 9. My lucky 7 places me on the cusp of living and dying. Not a particularly comfortable neighborhood to take up residence, but one in which I'm forced to live. During the operation to remove the prostate, my surgeon found that the cancer spread beyond the prostate gland and also into one of the lymph nodes. Three weeks after the operation we jointly decided what to do about it.

"You have two choices," he said.

"To live or to die?" I responded with gallows humor. I only became alarmed when he didn't smile.

"The first is waiting until the PSA number rises. A rising PSA indicates the cancer cells are growing. When it happens, we'll start female hormone therapy. The hormones will reduce your level of testosterone, which feeds the cancer cells."

"And the second?" I asked.

"To start immediately."

"Which has the best chance of killing the cancer?"

"Neither."

Neither? Although he kept talking, it was as if he was speaking an unintelligible foreign language. Eventually, I heard English again.

"Hormone therapy won't kill the cancer cells no matter when we start. It just prevents them from growing."

It was the first time I realized they'd be there forever, flowing through my body, waiting, and getting hungrier with time. They'd be back—not today or tomorrow, but someday.

"How effective is this form of therapy?" I asked.

"With your cancer, very effective. Most people I've been doing this with are alive ten years after we started."

"Ten years!" I said, sinking back into the chair. "That's not enough time. I'm only fifty-seven."

He told me the Mayo Clinic developed this protocol ten years ago. Since they had data only for that limited amount of time, nobody knew how long it would remain effective. I asked what would happen if the hormones didn't prevent the cells from growing.

"When that occurs, we'll try other therapies." His choice of the word "when" rather than "if" was frightening.

"If the drugs prevent them from growing, why would anyone wait?"

"The side effects."

"What am I going to do, grow breasts?" I asked.

"Not exactly," he said, again without smiling. "But your sex drive will be reduced. You'll gain weight. Some of your muscle will turn to fat. You'll have ten to thirty hot flashes every day. You'll become moody, and might have significant bone loss."

"You're describing menopause, aren't you?" I asked, remembering what my wife, Wendy, went through.

"Yes, but worse."

"Then why should I do it?"

"Because it's the only way of delaying the cells' growth." He explained that every three months I would receive a hormone injection and every six months a PSA test. When I asked for how long, he said, "Forever." Then, after a pause, "Or until it stops working."

"But you said it prevents the cells from growing?"

"Yes, for most people that's true."

I left his office realizing that even though the statistics were in my favor, I couldn't base my life on odds. I never hit a lottery ticket, beat the blackjack dealers in Las Vegas, or even won a raffle. What if I was one of the few who didn't respond to hormone therapy? And even if I did, he was clear that it couldn't be a cure. At best it was a holding action; something that might allow me to live long enough for another disease to kill me. My long-held belief that I controlled my life was obliterated by microscopic specks streaming through my blood and organs. And, as a university professor, the most frustrating thing was I couldn't reason with them!

Within two weeks of the first injection, I felt my body

changing. Nothing dramatic, rather, it was more like watching an overripe tomato start to rot. First came the hot flashes, then I gained weight, followed by exhaustion, and finally moodiness. As my life became more disrupted, I remembered the Tibetan saying that one should lean into the sharp points of life instead of running away. I had been running for three months from this sharp point. I tried to embrace the cancer with my heart, to "lean into it," as some of the literature suggested, and allow it to teach me about living. But how could I welcome something whose only purpose was to kill me?

The words I read, though meant to be spiritual, were hollow; devoid of anything comforting. I doubted anybody who developed cancer could honestly say they leaned into it. They'd pass me running away as fast as they could. My meditation practice, which had sustained me through many difficult times, couldn't measure up when the death I was contemplating wasn't theoretical or simulated within the safe confines of a workshop. This was my life, and the greatest wisdom from the most revered spiritual teacher would be just words.

Although friends and family tried to be compassionate, I felt they couldn't know what I was feeling. How can anyone understand what it's like living with a time bomb for the remainder of your life? Would today be the day the cancer decided to wake from hibernation? Or would it start growing next week, next month, or next year? My reluctance to talk about my feelings distanced me from everyone. I believed empathy wasn't possible unless the person was also living with a potentially terminal disease. I decided that other men with prostate cancer would be the ones who would best understand. I envisioned them as being part of a large brotherhood. I found a prostate cancer support group close to where I lived. When I told my family I would be attending, they seemed relieved.

I thought about the feelings I was having and was unable to discuss with anyone. How do I deal with the uncertainty of my life? How do I let go of things that define who I am? How can I accept what I've done and what I may never accomplish? How can I make amends to those I've offended before it's too late? I imagined the group members nodding their heads as I spoke and each eventually saying, "Yes, I know, I know," then providing me with the answers I desperately sought. With these anticipations I walked into my first meeting. It was then that I realized cancer affects each person differently. Some of the men were concerned about the effect the cancer was having on their sexual activities. Others were wrestling with their perceived lack of dignity because a loss of bladder control required them to wear absorbant briefs. A few felt that the word "cancer" changed how people viewed them, even though its early identification resulted in no physical problems. When it was my turn to speak, I couldn't ask any of those questions I was struggling with before the meeting. It had nothing to do with the people in the group. I realized they would be supportive no matter what I said. I just wasn't ready to display feelings that I hid since the diagnosis.

Instead of continuing with the group, I struggled alone, rereading how-to and inspirational books. Each was filled with vast amounts of information about cancer and consoling words about how to live with it. But, for me, the contents of these volumes seemed to represent wonderful theories of how things should be, rather than how things really were. The distance between what they described and my own life seemed unbridgeable. Clearly my response had nothing to do with the writing and everything to do with me. I needed something I could grasp and directly experience. And ultimately I found that "something," not through books or contemplation, but through a series of inexplicably related events that led me to children and adults who were dying. I didn't know why at the time, but I decided to become a bedside hospice volunteer.

It was a decision I couldn't expect my family or friends to understand—after all, I didn't understand it, and I rarely talked about it to anyone. I found it wasn't a welcome topic at social gatherings. People learned what I was doing when I would decline an invitation to do something on a Thursday night. When they asked why I couldn't come, and I responded with "I'll be doing my hospice shift then," my explanation was generally met with silence. To ask why I was choosing to be with people who were dying would draw attention to the possibility that my life might not be very long. Everyone knew the cancer had spread, and most people were afraid to ask how I was doing. Few were ready to discuss the real possibility that they might be losing me.

But there were some people who did want to know about my hospice experiences. We usually went off in a corner alone or met somewhere privately. I explained that hospice isn't a place—it's a state of mind, a willingness to compassionately accompany someone on their final journey, not judgmentally but as a friend who was willing to hold one's hand, cry, or just witness the end of life. As I walked that path with more than two hundred people, they became friends who led me into events that I had to face without any emotional armor. It was the first time in many years I felt authentic. These experiences reflected what's important in life more than could countless books and workshops. I watched the joy of a woman whose mouth was wired closed as she smelled a fragrant slice of apple, and I learned to accept what's possible rather than what's desired. I sat with a musician who was listening for the last time to a Grieg concerto, and I understood the beauty of things that had no words. As I played Chutes and Ladders with a child, I felt grief for the first time in my life and cried as he told me he knew this would be our last game.

Although every one of these people has died—these people who have taught me so much, my hospice teachers—this isn't a book about death. It's a blueprint for living. I participated in events so powerful they grabbed me and said, "Listen, this is important." When I paid attention, I felt a change. It was as if every time I left the bedside of a patient, I stepped into the crispness of a fall morning. Lucky people experience these transforming moments a few times throughout their lives. I feel so fortunate to have been able to experience these spiritual moments almost weekly for the past six years. I didn't become a hospice volunteer in order to accumulate information for this book. This book was an afterthought chronicling my experiences at the Zen Hospice Project's Guest House, George Mark Children's House, Maitri, Coming Home Hospice, Hospice By The Bay, and numerous facilities I was sent to as a volunteer by contracting agencies.

Sometimes the lessons had the impact of a sledgehammer, as when I was alone, holding a man with AIDS in my arms as he took his last breath. Other times, it was more subtle; after cradling a child for four hours, I realized he had synced his breathing with mine. From this intimacy with death came lessons, regardless of whether the teacher was six months old or someone who had witnessed the most important events of the last century. They unfolded when I allowed myself to develop a connectedness with the person I served—a willingness to see her or him as if it was me who was dying.

Most of the lessons I write about in this book, such as the power of forgiveness, may have sounded mundane to me until I saw the profound consequences that trying to be forgiven had for a lonely man whose last wish was to be forgiven by his brother. Other lessons, such as the importance of kindness, may have sounded like clichés to me, until I witnessed how a simple act infused with kindness overcame a woman's lifetime of misery and self-loathing. The lessons were immediate, often coming like a lightning strike. Understanding them was a different story. Some I quickly understood, but others alluded me, either because I needed to experience them as part of my own life or because their acceptance would have shattered my ego. But just as a stubborn puppy pulls on your pant leg until you acknowledge it, they remained just under my consciousness until I was ready for them. Despite trying to group them into some type of logical order for this book (such as "understanding, coping, and resolving"), I couldn't. I finally realized I was looking through a diamond, with each facet showing parts of all others. Each lesson therefore stands alone, although is connected to every other one.

It would have been wonderful if the lessons came in the order I needed them—like a how-to manual on living—but they didn't. A situation arose and there was a lesson! It didn't make any difference if I needed it then, three years before, or sometime in the future. Regardless of what was in the lesson, it was taught in the present; whether it was saying goodbye, coming to terms with the past, or giving up expectations for the future.

My entry into this intensive learning environment wasn't automatic. I was required to make a number of "attitude adjustments."

The first involved an expanded notion of truth that I learned from Linda, whom I was warned was a combative, but spiritually aware, person. When I entered her apartment and introduced myself, her eyes stopped at the Buddhist *mala*—a string of prayer beads like a Catholic rosary—on my wrist.

"Goldberg, right?" she said.

"Yes."

"Parents were Jewish?"

"Yes."

"From where?"

"Poland."

"And you were raised Jewish like me, weren't you?"

"I was."

"Then what's with the mala?"

"I was a philosophy major in college and I became interested in Buddhism. I feel a special kinship with Buddhist values."

"Do you eat meat?"

"Yes," I said. Seeing her look of disappointment, I added, "I'm not a perfect Buddhist."

"I knew it! You're a Jew-Bu."

"Excuse me?"

"Culturally, you're Jewish. By your accent, I think East Coast Jewish. Spiritually, your heritage goes back in time, maybe two thousand years, maybe even longer."

As I looked around her studio apartment I saw three statues of the Buddha, a cross, two *mahzuza*s (Jewish prayer scrolls within a silver container nailed on the entry of a house), a few books on Islam, the Hindu statue of Ghanesh, a very old copy of the Talmud written in Hebrew, and assorted Catholic rosaries. The abundance of objects from many religions reminded me of the story attributed to W. C. Fields, the great comedian of the 1930s and 1940s, who was an outspoken atheist. When he was dying, a friend came to visit and found Fields in bed reading the Bible. The shocked friend said, "Bill! What are you doing with that?" Fields looked up and said, "Insurance."

I initially thought Linda was the personification of the W. C. Fields story. But I quickly realized she wasn't. I stayed for four hours on that first visit, mostly listening. Linda talked as if she knew there wasn't much time left to share her ideas. She wasn't taking out insurance. It really didn't make a difference to her when and who said what, whether it was the Buddha, Christ, Gandhi, or the delivery person from Meals on

Wheels. Certain ideas were timeless for Linda, regardless of how they were clothed. I've tried to convey in this book those timeless ideas from my hospice experiences. You'll find them enveloped in the robes of a Buddhist monk, quietly enunciated through the solemnity of an Islamic saying, mounted on the precision of a Chinese philosophical thought, or embraced within the compassion of a basic Christian tenet.

The second adjustment I had to make involved touch. I had been the director of a speech-language clinic at a university, and one of my responsibilities was repeatedly to remind students not to touch clients. We were in a particularly litigious period in the 1980s, during which accusations of sexual abuse were being made against people who worked with children. So my instructions were "No touching of children, adolescents (especially adolescents!), or even adults." In hospice, I learned that touch was the most important human contact patients had with me and everyone else. It was an emotional bridge for them between life and death. When words stopped and hearing declined, they could still feel a human presence through my hands. There never was anything sexual with a hand affectionately held, a kiss, or even an embrace.

The third adjustment was learning that "it isn't about me." When someone became angry with me, or preferred another volunteer's company to mine, it was a statement about the person's needs, not a judgment about my abilities or personality. In hospice, the only person the world revolved around was the patient—not the person providing care.

The fourth and most difficult adjustment was explaining to friends and family how I saw my involvement in the lives of the people I served. For example, the first time I tried explaining my hospice work to a non-hospice friend, he suggested that I had the "Mother Teresa syndrome," meaning he felt that I had an extreme urge to be a rescuer, beyond what most people would feel or be capable of doing. How could I explain that the dynamics of hospice volunteering is so deeply compelling to many of us who do it that our involvement feels almost inevitable? There's a wonderful parable that illustrates what we as human beings do, because we're human. It goes like this: You're sitting and having a quiet conversation with a friend and you see a blind man walking toward the edge of a cliff. Your course of action would be simple and obvious, an expression of basic humanity—wouldn't you jump up and stop him before he stepped over the edge and fell to his death? To me, hospice is a perpetual cliff with an endless number of blind people walking to the edge. What I and thousands of other hospice volunteers do isn't heroic. The ability to be compassionate and attend to the needs of a dying person is part of our DNA—it's what we all are capable of doing when we look at another person as if they were ourselves.

Tibetan Buddhists believe in rebirth—and they refer to the experience between death and the next rebirth as the *bardo*. Although they use the term primarily to describe the time after death, I've found it to be equally applicable to any time or place where the "truths" we think are solid change into something the consistency of Jell-O. It is in that place of uncertainty where I have had the most insights. For me, being in the presence of people who are dying opened doors to wisdom I wouldn't have discovered through any other experience. My teachers (the hospice patients and staff) continually showed me how to stop looking for understanding and instead participate in the simplest things, from emptying an overflowing urinal to spooning ice cream into the mouth of someone who could no longer use his hands.

Nobody in hospice is just an observer—you can't be. Sometimes patients and their families ask you to do more than bear witness. Out of necessity you become involved. The scientist Jacob Bronowski wrote in his 1973 book *The Ascent of Man* that the world can only be grasped by action, not by contemplation.* I found that the same maxim applies to the understanding of my cancer, my life, and possibly my premature death.

In the fifteenth century, the Catholic Church produced a text called the *Ars moriendi* ("The Art of Dying"), which provided practical guidance for the dying and those attending them. *The Book of the Craft of Dying,* as it was called in its English translation, summarized in one sentence the lessons in this book:

> Learn to die and you shall live,
> for there shall be none
> who learn to truly live
> who have not learned to die.†

* From the *Ascent of Man* by Jacob Bronowski (New York: Little, Brown & Company).

† From *The Book of the Craft of Dying and Other Early English Tracts Concerning Death* by Francis M. M. Comper and Robert Kastenbaum (New York: Ayer, 1977).

1

Forgiveness

The quality of mercy is not strain'd.
It droppeth as the gentle rain from heaven
Upon the place beneath: it is twice blest;
It blesseth him that gives and him that takes.

—William Shakespeare

There is a presumption when you're asking for forgiveness that you did something wrong. Until the cancer, I was reluctant to ask for forgiveness. I might half-heartedly admit that I "misinterpreted," said something "without thinking it through," or any of a dozen other rationalizations that allowed me not to use the words, "Please forgive me." I didn't realize what asking for forgiveness really meant until I met Jim.

My first shift was scheduled for Thanksgiving at the Zen Hospice Project's Guest House, a hospice in San Francisco. Although I had the option of starting the following week, something compelled me to start then, even though it meant missing Thanksgiving with my family and friends. I spent the weekend before my shift amassing as many facts as I could.

That's how I tried making sense of things then; gathering information, numbers, and data. The book that had the greatest impact on me was *Final Gifts: Understanding the Special Awareness, Needs, and Communications of the Dying,* by the hospice-care nurses Maggie Callanan and Patricia Kelley. A recurring theme that Callanan and Kelley described about the experiences of people who were dying was their sense of embarking on a journey they said they were required to make, but for some reason couldn't start. One person talked about not having the key to open a locked door. A few people vividly described trips they were getting ready for but couldn't begin until something necessary, like a passport, was found. And others waited until they could say goodbye to someone. According to the authors, these were universal signals that something needed to be resolved before people allowed themselves to die. The idea that anyone could have control over the time of their death mystified me.

It was the Tuesday before Thanksgiving when I received an e-mail from the volunteer coordinator. Jim, one of the residents, was becoming confused, restless, and anxious. The coordinator asked if any volunteers could stay the night with him. Volunteer shifts normally end at 10:00 P.M. and with only one attendant on the floor at night, someone needed to be at his side from 10:00 P.M. to nine in the morning, when volunteers returned. Since I would already be there, I thought a few more hours wouldn't be a big deal. When I discussed it with my wife, Wendy, she asked if I was sure I wanted to do that, since this was my first hospice experience since completing my training.

"Of course," I responded. "What difference would a few more hours make?" I was still minimizing the lingering effects of the surgery and the perpetual exhaustion I felt from the cancer treatments. I could tell Wendy was concerned, but given our history (she usually wanted to discuss my feelings about the cancer and I usually refused) she didn't persist. I called the hospice attendant to let her know I would take the Thursday overnight shift.

"What can you tell me about Jim?" I asked.

"He's sixty-seven and was a heroin addict on and off since age seventeen," she said. "The last time he was using was about five years ago." There was a pause and I could hear her turning pages.

"I'm looking at his chart and see he doesn't get along with most people. Scares them actually. He's quiet during the day," she continued, "but at night he becomes a different person. We think it's the toxic chemicals his liver is producing. You know, he has hepatitis C."

I didn't expect that my first patient would be contagious and I would need to use every universal precaution I had been taught. Unfortunately, I didn't remember all of them. *How do you take the gloves off? Do you turn them inside out with a free pinky, or was it a thumb? What do you do if there is contact?* Until then, dealing with a contagious person was theoretical. *Yes, put on gloves, don't allow their bodily fluids to come in contact with your open sores, and wash your hands after you take off the gloves.* Since we spoke in generalities, it never was threatening. Now, it was someone with a name, whose body was home to a virus even more deadly than my cancer. And the only thing separating us would be a thin layer of latex and as much physical distance as I could create without being embarrassed.

"After ten, he enters another world," the attendant said. "Two things happened last night. The first was he left his room, yelling 'Deuce' as he walked through the House."

"Who's Deuce?"

"When I asked him, he said Deuce was his drug dealer. Then it got really strange. After I got him back into bed and left the room, he called me back and pleaded that I ask them to let him go."

"Who?" I asked.

"He said the bakery workers wouldn't let him leave because he hadn't finished baking something. In a loud voice I said, 'Let Jim leave!' It didn't help. He kept repeating that they won't let him leave until his bread was baked."

She continued talking, but I heard little. Not only did the story resonate with those from *Final Gifts*, but I remembered a conversation I had with the volunteer coordinator the previous week—I had offered to bake bread for the Thanksgiving dinner.

I drove to the House in the late afternoon on that warm Thanksgiving day. I parked at the end of the block and walked on a sidewalk covered with leaves, their normally brilliant colors muted by the overcast sky. The Guest House was a Victorian home that maintained its 1850s splendor while surrounded by similar houses that had seen their prime decades before. There was nothing on its exterior that hinted about the remarkable things occurring inside. The only sign was a small bronze plaque next to the front door that stated this was a historical building. In every pastel-painted room except the kitchen, chandeliers descended from high ceilings through plaster rosettes. The people who were cared for weren't called "patients," they were "residents," a distinction that was more than semantic. At capacity, six adults could be housed.

I opened the unlocked door and smelled roasting turkey. I saw about ten people, each doing something related to dinner. The living room was transformed into a festive dining area with a large table in the center, covered with a purple tablecloth that shimmered as you passed by it. In the center was a beautiful flower arrangement, more glorious than anything in *House and Garden*, and on the mantel were at least forty cards with names written in calligraphy. *Forty?* I didn't realize there would be that many at the meal. As I wondered if I baked enough bread, people greeted me. Some I knew, others were staff I'd seen but never met. An older woman, wearing a colorful vest that was probably vintage 1970s, offered to take the bread into the kitchen. It was still warm, and the smell stunned her. She called other people over to share the experience. One was a resident who had non-Hodgkin lymphoma. He was a huge man with letters tattooed on each of his fingers, from when he had been in San Quentin; sideburns down to his jawline; and a straggly mustache. I expected a deep rumbling to come out of his mouth, but his voice was amazingly soft as he told me his name, Paul, and then he introduced me to June, his wife. Although shorter than Paul, June blocked out his silhouette when she stepped in front of him. She immediately embraced me in a bear hug, kissing me as if I was a favorite nephew.

When June released me and moved to the side, I saw someone insisting on walking down from the second floor. His gaunt face was covered by a gray mustache and beard, his long thinning hair was tied in a ponytail, and his jeans were bunched in the front so they wouldn't fall off. After four steps, he couldn't move. Exhausted, he slowly sank onto a stair. It brought back memories of walking down the stairs in my house for the first time after surgery, each step sending a sharp pain through my body.

"Jim, would you like help coming down?" the woman in the vest asked from downstairs.

With his eyes closed and his upper body held upright by two volunteers, he nodded his head yes. They raised him and using a fireman's carry brought him down the remaining ten steps. After they gently lowered Jim into a wheelchair, he rested his chin on his chest. When his breathing slowed, he was wheeled into the dining room and a chair next to where I sat was removed. The table had twelve place settings precisely laid out as if on a grid. I wondered where the other twenty-eight people were and where they would sit. I waited for Jim to turn in my direction, but he didn't.

"Hi Jim," I finally said. The disease had so ravaged him, he was unable to move his head. He turned his upper body to see me, and our eyes met. He stared without blinking, without expressing anything. I thought his look was imploring me to say or do something. But what? The best I could say was, "I'm Stan. I'll be staying with you through the night. This is my first shift at the House, so if I screw up, please let me know."

He leaned toward me and in a barely audible voice said,

"There's no way you can make as many mistakes as I have. Don't sweat it."

Shortly afterward, the remaining ten people sat down and someone suggested we remember those who died at the Guest House over the past few months. He gestured toward the place cards on the mantel. During the silent meditation period, I didn't think about the names. Instead, memories of my parent's deaths flashed back along with frightening images of what my own might look like. After we finished, Jim turned back to his food and tried to pick up a fork. Although he could hold it, his fingers didn't have the strength to grasp it firmly and it dropped to the floor. The person next to him, who was talking to someone across the table, took another fork without stopping his conversation and picked up a small amount of sweet potatoes. As he raised it, Jim opened his mouth and smiled at the volunteer. I looked around the table and saw nobody showed any interest in what was occurring; almost as if this was common.

After eating a few bites of sweet potatoes and some ice cream, Jim slowly hunched over. Was he dying right here in front of me? No one seemed concerned until someone casually asked him if he would like to go back to his room. He nodded yes, and was wheeled to the steps. Four people lifted the chair with Jim in it and gently carried him upstairs. My family and friends were joyfully feasting on turkey and listening to our annual playing of Arlo Guthrie's "Alice's Restaurant," a song in which the joy of a Thanksgiving meal turns into a bizarre adventure. I was in the middle of one, sharing food with people who were dying and had diseases that could kill me.

It was about eight when dinner was over. Paul and June went back upstairs to their room. Everyone else spontaneously started clearing the table. When I entered the kitchen, someone was doing dishes and another person was wrapping the food for tomorrow's meals. Everyone left except the attendant, Evan, and one other volunteer, Gary. Evan went upstairs to be with the residents while Gary and I finished cleaning. When we were done, we were expected to go upstairs and spend time with the residents. When I asked the volunteer coordinator before my shift began what I should be doing, she said, "Just be present." Although I nodded, signaling that I understood, I didn't.

I would be with Jim throughout the night, and Gary would stay with the other two residents until ten. Paul's wife would be taking care of him, and Evan would be there for everyone. Attendants were very special people. Some were certified nurses assistants (CNAs), and others had slightly less training; although I never could tell the difference in their duties. The residents referred to them as "angels." Whatever was needed by the residents they did; from changing soiled linens to monitoring medications to quietly sitting by the bedside holding someone's hand as he or she died.

I realized I was repeatedly vacuuming the same spot on the rug, dragging out the cleaning as long as I could. Downstairs, there was distance between Jim and me. It felt safe, and now, very clean. Upstairs, well, I didn't know how I was going to be "present."

As I climbed the stairs, the food odors faded, gradually overpowered by the smell of disinfectant. I asked Evan for the notes kept on each resident. I read that Jim only left his room when he had the strength. Since the prior week, he had been downstairs just once. Only a few people had come to visit since he arrived two months ago. And he was becoming combative and increasingly incontinent. Bowel movements were loose because of the colitis, and he often couldn't get to the commode in time, or, when he was delirious, he forgot to take off his pants and diaper.

I entered Jim's room and saw him sitting on a recliner with his eyes closed. According to Evan, Jim hadn't slept in his bed for two days. He preferred to sleep fully clothed on the recliner. I looked at the bed with its quilt and puffed-up pillows, trying to imagine how many people died in it over the seventeen-year existence of the Guest House and wondering if the number would increase that night.

"Hi Jim," I said, sitting in a chair three feet away from him. He said something, but I couldn't hear what it was. I moved the chair closer and said, "Is there anything I can get you?"

He shook his head no.

"Anything I can do for you?"

Again, a no. I noticed he was wearing dress shoes covering socks whose elastic tops were indenting his skin. "Those shoes and socks look uncomfortable. Would you like me to take them off?" I asked.

He shook his head no, then slowly turned to me and waited until I moved even closer. Reluctantly, I placed my ear a few inches from his mouth and wondered if he'd spray me with saliva. And if he did, how would I react? I prepared to pull away as he started speaking.

"They pinch my toes," he said, barely above a whisper.

"If they pinch your toes, why don't you want them off?"

"It keeps me awake."

I didn't know if he wanted to stay awake because he feared dying if he fell asleep, or because he wanted to talk. If it was the first, I didn't think I was ready for it. If it was the second, I would be less concerned, but unsure how to talk to him. Despite the role playing we did in training, I felt like a teenager about to meet a blind date. Our conversation began easily enough with me asking him how long he had been at the House. He said three months. He asked me how long I had been doing this. I said, "Since dinner." He laughed. But as his laugh changed into a cough, I held my breath. When he finally stopped, I inhaled.

For a while, the easy talk continued. I asked how he liked the food. He said, "It depends upon who's cooking." He asked me how old I was. I said almost fifty-eight. Then after some more small talk came a shift in the conversation's tone when I asked him how old he was. "I'm sixty-seven and won't see sixty-eight." I tried changing the direction of the conversation. As a new hospice volunteer, I still wasn't comfortable talking about death. I asked how long he lived on the streets. "More than anyone should have to," he said. He was as persistent as a telemarketer trying to get you to buy penny stocks. I realized that no matter what I would say, he would pull me back to what he wanted to talk about, not just the facts of his life, which on their own were frightening enough, but most likely how he was feeling about his dying. Reluctantly, I gave in and asked about his pain. He told me with enough morphine, even the worst eventually went away. I nodded my head, agreeing.

"How do you know about morphine?" he asked.

"I have prostate cancer. They gave it to me last year after surgery."

Jim wanted to know if I had family. Yes, I said. A wife and two adult children. I was no longer holding my breath as he spoke, and my chair was now touching the recliner. We were speaking with just inches separating our heads when he fell asleep. Earlier, I read in the notes he often did this—fell asleep, eyes wide open, then started speaking when he woke as if there never was an interlude. I sat and waited.

Ten minutes later he said, "How old?"

"My son's twenty-two and my daughter's twenty-six."

"How did you tell them about the cancer?"

Although it had been a year, I still wasn't comfortable talking about those conversations.

"It was hard," was all I said.

Jim kept looking at me as if he were waiting for more. I saw his eyes were glistening.

"Do you have any kids?" I asked. One girl, he told me, who hadn't visited. Jim didn't think his daughter knew he was dying.

"I haven't seen her in five years. She's in Illinois."

"Would you like to see her?"

As he nodded his head yes, the hints of moisture tipped out, forming thin streams that cascaded only an inch or so down his checks.

"Can anyone get in touch with her?"

"Her mother, but she won't do it. They don't speak. We don't speak." There was a long pause, and then he said, "I need to ask her to forgive me."

I asked him if he would like us to see if we could contact his daughter. With closed eyes he nodded his head yes, then slowly exhaled. When he fell asleep, I went outside the room and asked Evan if Jim ever talked about his daughter.

"No," he said. "This is significant. I'll see what I can find out after my shift is over. Then we'll try to call her."

I went back into the room and sat next to Jim as he slept. I thought about the times when I could have sabotaged my relationship with my children. I remembered when my son was nine and I had been under stress. I was directing a university program and enlarging my private practice. Between the two, I had little time for my family. As my son and I were walking together on a busy street near our house, he reached up and grabbed my hand. My thought was to withdraw it, and lecture him that nine-year-olds don't hold their father's hand in public. When I looked down at this face, I realized he was using a physical connection to compensate for the emotional one I was denying him. I held his hand tighter and turned away before he saw my tears. What if I had withdrawn my hand? Would Justin have become as distant as it appeared Jim's daughter was from him? And if I had rejected him, how would I ask Justin, as an adult, to forgive me? I wondered how Jim would do it. What could have happened to make a daughter not want to have contact with her father for five years? And would the knowledge her father was dying be enough to overcome it?

Jim woke again and for the next three hours we talked as

if we were lifelong friends sitting at a bar, delighted just to be with each other. Maybe this is what "being present" meant. He told me how he loved to sing classical music, but that he could barely breathe anymore. I told him about my love of fly-fishing in remote areas, but because of my hormone treatments I was too weak to go alone. Climbing steep canyons was no longer possible. Walking was even painful since I fractured my pelvis playing handball. I asked him if he'd like me to make French toast in the morning from the bread I baked. There was a long pause and then he slowly turned so he was looking directly at me.

"You bake bread?"

"Yes, I do."

"What kind?"

"Well, for tonight's dinner I baked challah, egg bread."

"Can you get me the recipe?"

"Sure, I'll bring it in next week."

He leaned back on the recliner, remaining silent for about a minute, then turned toward me, inhaling as much as he could to complete another sentence. "I want to make that bread, but I know I can't."

"We'll do it together," I said with a quivering voice.

He closed his eyes, smiled, and then fell asleep. As I watched him, death became more real and frightening. The real thing was in front of me in a body that was winding down and a brain that couldn't tell delusion from reality. I wondered if this is how I would die; watching my abilities fall away to the point where I couldn't even feed or wipe myself. My apprehension stopped when he woke.

"I'm hungry," Jim said.

Thank God! At least here's something simple. Something I could do without thinking. After all, how difficult will it be to feed someone?

"What would you like?" I asked.

"Ice cream."

"I'll go downstairs and see if there's any left."

The mantra at the Guest House was there are no emergencies in hospice. I was told people were there to die, not recover. In a hospital there is a sense of urgency when a life is in jeopardy. Here, everything moved slowly, deliberately, as if each moment was to be savored. But I forgot the mantra and painfully bounded down the stairs, each step reminding me my reduced bone density was putting me at risk for another fracture. In the freezer were quart containers of chocolate and vanilla. Plenty to satisfy the small amount I thought he would eat. I ran back up.

"There's chocolate and vanilla. Which do you want?"

"Both."

I went back down and put a large scoop of each in a bowl and again climbed the stairs.

"I have both in this bowl. Which one would you like to start with?"

"Both."

I took a small portion of each on a spoon. "I'm going to feed you, so let me know if the amount is too large."

He nodded his head, and I slowly placed the spoon into his open mouth. He closed it, allowing the ice cream to slide off as I pulled out the spoon. His eyes closed, and he slowly moved his tongue from side to side. With each movement of his tongue, his smile grew. Sometimes it took thirty seconds before the ice cream was gone and he was ready for the next spoonful. It was something so simple, so pleasurable, I couldn't understand it. Pleasure for me had always been complicated. I felt it when I made a perfect cast to a fish hidden behind a rock as I stood in my favorite stream in Wyoming. I experienced it completing a poem in which I merged thoughts into a unified line. But that night, it was just the taste of ice cream that seemed to bring more joy to someone than I could have ever experienced through complex manipulations of either my body or mind. We repeated the sequence for the next ten minutes until the bowl was empty.

"More please," he whispered.

I went downstairs, refilled the bowl, and we began again. After he finished, I sat next to him and tried to sleep when he did, propping my feet on a second chair. Shortly after one o'clock I felt a tapping on my shoulder and woke. Irma, the late-night attendant, introduced herself. She gave Jim a dose of Roxanol, a liquid derivative of morphine.

"Lie down on the couch," the tiny older woman then said to me. She was less than five feet tall, and she spoke quietly, with a South American accent. "You sleep. He'll go to sleep now." I later learned that Irma had come to San Francisco from Bolivia forty years earlier, when she was in her mid-thirties. Most of us at the hospice thought of Irma as the caring grandmother we all dreamed of having.

"But if I sleep over there," I said, pointing to the couch on the other side of the room, "I won't hear him if he wakes."

"Don't worry. I'll be here," she said.

She pulled a blanket and pillow from a second bed in the alcove and placed them on the floor between the recliner where Jim slept and the door. She had been doing this since the previous week when Jim began wandering. He would often wake and try to walk quietly down the stairs. Irma couldn't watch him and take care of the other residents by herself. That's why people had volunteered to stay with him throughout the night—every night until he died.

"Sleep, sleep," Irma said to me. I didn't need any encouragement. She lay on the floor and I crunched sideways on the couch with a blanket pulled up to my head. I almost immediately fell asleep.

"I need your help," Irma said in a whisper, as she gently tapped my shoulder. I looked at the clock. It had been less than an hour. "I'm sorry, but he's had an accident."

Although I was groggy, I knew what she meant. I reached into my back pocket and pulled out the gloves. Across the room I saw Jim.

"I'm sorry, I'm sorry," he said, standing next to the recliner. "Goddamn it. Look what I did," he said, staring at his soiled jeans.

Earlier in the evening I wondered how I would react to cleaning another person, especially someone contagious. Worse, would it be a preview of my future? Looking at Jim apologizing over and again, my fears and the odor that filled the room both disappeared. In their place, I saw someone devastated by probably one of the most embarrassing things an adult can do in the presence of other people.

"I'm sorry, I'm sorry. Look what I did," he repeated.

"It's all right Jim," I said.

Irma and I helped him to the bed, where it would be easier to clean him. He stopped apologizing as she told him where to move his legs and what we would be doing. Irma directed each of my movements like a choreographer preparing a child for his first dance recital. When I hesitated, she would gently take my hands and place them where she wanted them.

It took almost thirty minutes to clean him, change his clothes, and replace the bed linens. When we began, my hands moved hesitantly, almost as if my fears pulled them back. But when I stopped trying to analyze everything and just let my concern for him lead me, a flowing rhythm developed. I didn't have to wonder if I was rubbing him too roughly or too lightly. It was as if I were transported back to when I changed my children's diapers, and my hands instinctively knew what to do.

Finally done, I slept on the couch until six when Jim woke. He asked to go back to the recliner, and I gently led him there. He turned his body so he could look out the window on the other side of the room. It was a typical gray San Francisco morning.

"It's going to be a good day," he said, then fell back to sleep.

Evan came to the House at 8:00 A.M. even though his shift didn't start until late afternoon. He stood outside Jim's room and motioned to me. We walked down the hall so Jim wouldn't hear us.

"I asked the house manager about Jim's daughter," he whispered.

"Can we contact her?" I asked.

"No."

"Why not? He wants to see her."

"She said she died five years ago."

"But we talked about a daughter in Illinois. Are you sure there isn't another one?"

"No. That was Jim's only child. She's buried there. The family blames him for his daughter's death. Nobody here knows how it happened, and the family didn't want to talk about it."

At 9:00 A.M., after spending eighteen hours at the Guest House, I left to go home. The street seemed cleaner, the sky bluer, and I was becoming less afraid of my emotions. I confronted my fears of contagion and death that night, not by talking but by doing. I was experiencing Jim's dying, and I was imagining what might happen to me. I wondered if he agreed with his family and blamed himself? I was so overwhelmed by my experiences that I had to concentrate on remembering to stop at traffic lights and stay on the right side of the road as I drove. I felt as if I were dropped from a sensory deprivation chamber into the middle of a Rolling Stones concert. Only ten minutes more, then I'd be home.

"How was it?" Wendy asked as I walked through the door. I couldn't speak. I started to cry and hugged her as my grown children looked on. After my night with Jim, I felt more alive than I ever had. During my shift, there wasn't time to think about the past or future. My mind remained in the present, unlike the previous six months, which I had spent wallowing in the past—trying to relive experiences that I would never have again—or leaping into the future, creating goals that would affirm a long life—one that I might not have. For the next three weeks, I stayed overnight every Thursday after the end of my shift. One week, I stayed overnight on two consecutive days. Although there were peaceful times, Jim was acutely agitated at least half of the time. One night, he even tried to punch Irma when she was giving him morphine.

"Is that the best you can do?" he shouted as I caught a left hook before it could hit her face. I don't remember ever reacting so fast.

"Jim, it's me, Irma," she said to him sweetly, not flinching. Their faces were inches from each other as I struggled to hold back his arm. Instead of moving away, Irma kept talking. "Remember? You said I was like a grandmother to you. Remember?"

He looked at her intently. Finally, there was a look of recognition, then he said, "Hey, Irma. How are you, darling?" A smile came over his face, and I felt his muscles relax. Then I watched his eyes close.

This pattern repeated itself for the next few weeks. Jim became agitated, believing he was on the streets again, ready to fight all comers whether they were imaginary street people trying to steal his stash or the little Bolivian grandmother who was trying to comfort him. When the delusions stopped, and if he was conscious, he apologized profusely, repeatedly asking everyone in the room to forgive him. As he ate less, his body began consuming its own fat, revealing a wiry, muscular physique. If you didn't know his condition, you might assume he was an aging boxer. Then, with little fat left, his muscle started breaking down.

Volunteers agreed to stay at his bedside twenty-four hours a day. The nurse told me the toxic chemicals his dying liver was producing caused the agitation. I thought it was more than chemistry. He struggled constantly with things that needed finishing before he died. His comment at Thanksgiving dinner that I could never make as many mistakes as he did was the first sign. Then came the conversation about wanting to reestablish a connection with his daughter. As our friendship developed, he talked about wanting to ask for forgiveness from scores of people he hurt. Some had already died; others he didn't know about. Family, other than his brother, wouldn't speak to him.

Whatever mistakes Jim made in the past didn't appear correctable, or, if they were, I couldn't seem to help him find a way to do it. Perhaps I didn't have the experience, or the wisdom, or the willingness to open myself even more than I had already. The only thing I could do was listen. Other volunteers were more successful at calming Jim than I was. One woman got in bed with him when nothing helped the pain and restlessness. She caressed him until he fell asleep, the way a mother caresses a frightened child. I was humbled watching her, wondering if I could ever become as compassionate. But even with her, Jim's agitation stopped only for short periods. Few friends visited. After repeated phone calls from Jim to his brother, he agreed to come and stay with him for two days. When he heard his brother would be visiting, we talked about forgiveness. He wanted to ask for it, but was afraid to.

I never saw Jim's brother smile, and I never saw him talk to any of the volunteers or staff. During the first day of his stay, I heard their conversation through the open door of his room. It started pleasantly, with both of them recollecting their childhoods, then adolescence, and finally adulthood. As they progressed through the years, joviality was gradually replaced by accusations. He reminded Jim of every thoughtless thing he ever did, using words that sounded to me as if they were burning the inside of his mouth. He sank lower into the recliner as his brother vividly described painful events for twenty minutes.

Tearfully he said, "I'm sorry, Rick, please forgive me. I'm sorry for the pain I caused you."

"Really? You should have thought about it before you went back to using."

"I know."

"Even if I forgive you, your daughter is still dead because of you."

I didn't hear any words indicating that he was shocked. I had wondered since our first night if he really believed his daughter was still alive. When he started crying, Rick left the room. I entered quietly and sat next to him.

"It didn't work," he said. "I've done some terrible things in my life," he continued.

"We all have."

"No, you don't understand. You can't. Not bad things. Terrible things. There are things I can't be forgiven for. I know that when I die, people will celebrate. And they should. I wanted my brother to forgive me, but I didn't think he would. Actually, I knew he wouldn't, but I had to try."

As he cried, I put my arm around him. I had never done

that with Jim. Hugging and cradling were things he always wanted from female volunteers. Firm handshakes were for men. As I held him, he leaned toward me. This was the closest we had ever been physically. I started thinking about things I did throughout my life that I was sorry for. The list seemed endless. Eventually he became quiet.

Looking at me he said, "You're a sweetheart."

"That's not something I'd expect to hear from a street-smart guy like you. I don't even hear that from my wife," I lied. He laughed. We were both becoming more comfortable expressing our feelings. "Is there anything I can do for you, Jim?"

In a clear voice, he said, "Shoot me."

"Sorry. Anything, but that," I said. He smiled and leaned back in the recliner waiting for the morphine to take effect.

I knew he would be in physical and psychological pain until he died. I didn't admit it to anyone, but I hoped it would happen soon. I saw aspects of Jim's life in my own. I looked back on times when I wanted to ask for forgiveness but didn't. I wondered if my father's death twenty-five years ago would have been any different if I had been able to ask him to forgive some spiteful things I said years before he died. Would his last few hours have been more peaceful if I were able to express gratitude for all he gave me? I was slightly better with my mother's death. I always wondered if she knew how important she was to me. I knew I should have told her, but I wasn't able to then.

I was spending Tuesday and Thursday overnights with Jim. But one Thursday in December, all the volunteers were required to attend a training session at another location. The first presentation was by a nurse who had been working in hospice for fifteen years. As she described her interactions with patients, I realized I still wasn't able to deal with an idea that had been presented during my training: being able to fall in love with those I served and then let them go without regrets. I wouldn't say I'd fallen in love with Jim. Maybe I felt the type of friendship that occurs when you share experiences so wrenchingly authentic that they create a bond that defines the relationship forever. I knew I would miss him like a crotchety old uncle who, years after his death, is only remembered for his good qualities.

"How do you accept the loss when someone you love dies?" I asked.

She immediately replied, "Love can take many forms. The love I experience for my patients involves feeling I've done everything I could have to make their death as peaceful as possible. I knew every one of the thousands I cared for would die within six months. If I focused on that, I'd go crazy or quit. But when you know you're helping them on a journey, your love is different. So is your sense of loss. Yes, I miss most of the patients I've worked with, but that's minor compared with what I think I gave them."

There was another speaker, but at the end of the nurse's presentation, I began feeling intense pains in my abdomen. Even though my surgeon had told me that when the cancer returns it wouldn't give me dramatic pain, I excused myself and left anyway, feeling a little panicked.

The next morning I received an e-mail announcing that Jim had died at nine o'clock the previous night. I realized my pains began shortly afterward. I had never believed in prophetic feelings. Those that I had experienced, I always credited to coincidence. When other people would tell me about theirs, I would listen politely and think, "Give me a break! Who could believe that?" Now I don't question them.

The e-mail said his body would be removed from the House at eleven in the morning. Anyone who would like to say goodbye could sit with him until then. I arrived at nine and sat alone at the side of the bed. It was the first time I saw him looking peaceful. I felt I was looking at the face of a sixty-seven-year-old baby, content to just be. When I went home, I reread one of my favorite passages from the Buddha's teachings:

> This existence of ours is as transient as autumn colds.
> To watch the birth and death of beings
> is like looking at the movements of a dance.
> A lifetime is like a flash of lightning in the sky,
> rushing by, like a torrent down a steep mountain.*

After Jim died, I asked my wife and children to forgive me for a number of thoughtless things I had done. Fortunately, they weren't in the same league with the death of Jim's daughter, but I often ask myself, *What if they were?* How could I ask for forgiveness for something that was "terrible"? I'm not sure I could, although after Jim, I was inspired to help other

* From the Diamond Sutra, in Sogyal Rinpoche, *The Tibetan Book of Living and Dying* (New York: HarperSanFrancisco, 1994), 25.

people do the same thing. I helped one woman write a letter asking for forgiveness from her adult daughter, whom she felt she had neglected as a child. For another patient, a phone call to an answering machine was all he could do. It seems to me that asking for forgiveness is redemptive, not necessarily in any religious sense, but it seems to remove something that makes the journey more difficult.

There's an old Buddhist story about a monk who would walk around with two bags of pebbles tied to his waist. One bag contained white pebbles and the second, black ones. Whenever he did something virtuous he took out a white pebble and put it in his pocket. Whenever he did something that was hurtful to someone, he took out a black one. At the end of the day he looked at the number of white and black pebbles in his pocket. If the whites outnumbered the blacks, it was a good day. Since seeing the pain of someone who desperately wants forgiveness before they die, I understand how important it is to ask now—and to forgive others now, too. I've found that when I ask for forgiveness for something I did that was thoughtless, some of my black stones magically become white.

2

Letting Go

> Although we have been made to believe that
> if we let go we will end up with nothing, life
> itself reveals again and again the opposite:
> that letting go is the path to real freedom.
>
> —Sogyal Rinpoche

Like so many other people, I always believed that if I let go of things, I'd be left with nothing. This was especially true when it came to my physical abilities. Even though my body was aging, before the cancer it still was a friend. I could keep up with my adult son on long runs, outpace him when we rode our bikes together, and rarely asked for his help to lift anything lighter than fifty pounds. But the words "prostate cancer" and its treatment effects caused me to cling even more tightly to an image of who I had once been. I had done wilderness backpacking, completed one-hundred-mile bike races, fly-fished in remote areas, run marathons, and canoed by myself in the backwaters of the Everglades.

I was what I did. These were parts of my identity I refused to let go of, even as the hormone treatments sent undeniable signals to me that I shouldn't be doing these things anymore, or at least not by myself. I knew my insistence on acting as if nothing had changed was worrying everyone in my family and most of my friends. When will Dad fall into a ravine again? Will it be more than a pelvis fracture the next time he hits a wall playing handball? And will the Coast Guard inform us that he drowned during one of his swims in San Francisco Bay?

Many of the things I thought necessary for making life meaningful were being taken away. It was as if an expanding sinkhole developed in the center of my identity. Although I had the love of my family and friends, an intact mind, and few financial worries, I could only focus on what I lost and what I might continue to lose. Acceptance of the new me was unfathomable. How could I let go of what gave me pleasure throughout my life? When everything was gone, who would I be then? These questions were answered when I met Cindy.

"There are so many of you," Cindy wrote on the small erasable slate outlined with yellow plastic flowers. She was referring to the number of volunteers. For each five-hour shift at the Guest House, two of us were upstairs with the residents. Sometimes another was downstairs cooking.

"I know," I said. "We multiply like bunnies."

Cindy tried to laugh, but only the right side of her face and lips moved upward. She was one year younger than I, and she had come with her mother, Anna, to live at the hospice. Two years earlier, a surgeon had removed her cancerous pharynx and tongue and created a stoma, which is an opening in the front of the throat to breathe. Neither food nor water could pass through her mouth, since it would enter her lungs and suffocate her. To prevent that, the surgeon had also wired her mouth closed.

During the first two weeks of her stay at the Guest House, Cindy was alert enough to communicate through gestures and her erasable slate. She didn't need to do much; often a look was sufficient. Eye contact with me and a movement of her head toward Anna meant she wanted to write without her mother present.

"Anna, why don't you take a break? You can have a cup of tea downstairs," I said. "Cindy and I will be fine together."

"Are you sure?" Anna asked.

Cindy gestured toward her mother, as if shooing a child out of a room. After she left, Cindy shook her head and picked up her plastic pen. By the second week, it was difficult for her to hold it.

"Lonely when I go," she haltingly wrote on the slate, then quickly erased it.

"I know. We're all doing whatever we can to prepare her. I think the social worker is trying to find a support group for when you leave."

She laid her head on her pillow, then straightened her blanket so it neatly draped over her body, which had lost a significant amount of muscle and most fat. When I first met her, she weighed less than one hundred pounds, one-third of her weight before the cancer. When people visited, she would move the blankets and bend her legs at the knee so their outline wouldn't show. She also tried to keep the stoma covered and constantly dabbed at it so phlegm wouldn't be visible. When it was time to give her nutrients through the feeding tube going into her stomach, she had her mother ask everyone except the attendant to leave.

On one shift Cindy told me that what she missed most was the crunch of an apple. When I returned the following week, I greeted her and sat down next to her without saying anything. She always wanted me immediately to tell her what I did during the week, how my family was, and if I wrote anything new. She gestured to me as if saying, "Are you going to talk to me, or what?" Instead of saying anything, I kept looking into a brown paper bag I brought with me. Finally, I smiled, pulled out an apple and carefully cut two slices from it. As I moved one slice toward her, she looked confused until I placed it under her nose. As she started to smell it, I put the other slice into my mouth. Simultaneously, I chewed while she sniffed. After a few bites, I stopped eating and watched her expression as the tension in her face and body melted away with each inhale.

When I entered the room the following week, I saw her with a telephone to her ear. She tapped three times on the mouthpiece with her pen and tried to smile. I looked to Anna for an explanation.

"She's on the phone with Tom," Anna said. "He calls her every day with a joke and she tells him how funny she thinks it is by the number of taps. A three isn't very good."

I learned that Tom was a volunteer with another hospice agency that took care of Cindy when she and Anna were still living in their one-bedroom apartment. His daily calls continued into the third week of Cindy's refusing to take any more nourishment through her feeding tube.

In hospice, wishes are respected, whether it involves something trivial like positioning flowers or something as serious as refusing food. As I sat next to her, holding her hand while her mother tried to convince her to again take nourishment, I wondered if my family would do the same with me, and if I would be able to make a decision, as Cindy did, that would shorten my life.

"I think she may want to start taking nutrition again," Anna said. "I don't think the nurse is listening. I think she's changed her mind."

"Why don't I ask her to talk with Cindy and you again?" I offered.

"Please."

Cindy was firm. She didn't want any nutrients, only extra morphine to control the pain. Even as Cindy dramatically declined, Anna kept praying for a miracle to save her daughter's life. Votive candles filled their room, each showing a picture of a different saint.

"For two years," Anna said to me as she lit a candle, "I did whatever was necessary."

"I know," I said, looking at Cindy, who was sleeping.

Volunteers on every shift spent hours trying to help Anna accept that Cindy was dying. As Cindy became less alert, Anna's apprehension increased. She refused to leave the room unless a volunteer sat at her daughter's side. We couldn't always help, because shifts ended at 10:00 P.M. After that, Anna was alone with Cindy and the attendant until 9:00 A.M. For eleven hours Anna sat in a chair next to Cindy, drifting in and out of sleep throughout the night. When it was quiet, the attendant relieved Anna for a few hours, allowing her to sleep on the couch on the other side of the room.

The discoloration beneath Anna's eyes darkened, and a slight tremor developed in her left hand. The call went out for volunteers to stay through the night. I stayed with them for five nights during the next two weeks. When Anna was awake, we talked about Cindy's eventual death and what Anna would do then. They were difficult conversations for both of us. I prayed that as Cindy came closer to her death, Anna would be more accepting of it. Through the beginning of the third week without nutrition that didn't happen. I hoped my family would do better if my health deteriorated. "I need to offer more prayers," Anna said as she lit three new candles. Every flat surface in the room was filled with flickering lights, creating a sweet odor that permeated the entire house. If one went out, Anna immediately relit it, as if not doing so would hasten Cindy's death. I asked Anna to come out of Cindy's room so we could talk.

"Anna, you know it's getting close, don't you?"

"Yes, I know," she said, with tears flowing from puffy eyes. "But I don't want her to go."

"I think she knows that. And I know she's more worried about you than her pain."

"I know."

We were trained to be compassionate listeners. To be present with residents and their families. We were to be companions to the dying. As someone who spent a lifetime counseling people with communication problems, it was difficult for me not to be directive. But I felt my experience with grief and loss didn't warrant "should" suggestions, despite knowing Cindy's feelings. During my conversations with her, I learned Cindy's primary concern was Anna's well-being. I felt Cindy was holding on to life, regardless of the pain, until Anna could accept her death. The conversation I wanted to have was one in which I would suggest to Anna that she tell Cindy how much she meant to her and even give Cindy permission to die. As much as I wanted to suggest that, I didn't. Instead, I asked questions.

"Anna, have you told Cindy how much she means to you and how much you'll miss her?" I thought of my wife and wondered what she would say to me when it was my turn.

"She knows that."

"But have you told her?" I thought of the last words I would have with my children.

"No. If I do, she'll know she's dying."

I knew Cindy was aware she was dying long before they came to the Guest House. I said, "When people are dying, they often continue to stay until certain things are finished."

"I don't understand," she said.

"You know Cindy is in pain although the morphine dosage was increased."

"Yes."

"Cindy and I talked about how hard it will be for you when she dies." There was a long pause as Anna began to realize what my earlier statement might mean. When she did, Anna began to sob.

"Do you think she's staying because of me?"

I didn't say anything. When Anna's quiet sobs became louder, we walked down the hallway so Cindy wouldn't hear.

"When my husband died, I accepted it," she said. "He lived a long life. But this is my little girl."

"I know."

"How can I tell my child it's all right to die?"

I didn't have an answer then, nor do I now, even after caring for scores of children and adults who left behind parents. I've talked with friends who had to make the decision to stop life support for their child, and I also held parents' hands as they found the words that allowed their children to leave. I was in awe of what they did and felt absolute terror at the thought of being forced to do the same thing.

I didn't see Anna and Cindy for a few days. When I returned to the House, Cindy's condition had worsened so dramatically that caring for her physical needs was a problem. During the previous five weeks of her stay, Cindy allowed only female volunteers to be present when her clothes or bed linens were changed. But without any nutrients she grew weaker, and her modesty became an issue. She weighed less than ninety pounds, and with atrophied muscles it was difficult for her to move or remain in a position for the attendant to clean or change her. Anna often didn't have the strength to hold Cindy. As the health of both mother and daughter continued to decline, modesty was sacrificed.

"Stan, could you help me change Cindy?" Martha, the attendant, asked.

"It's okay Cindy," Anna quickly said. "Don't be embarrassed, it's Stan."

Cindy turned and smiled at me. She didn't need any reassurance. We had become close friends. When we were together, I used words and she, gestures and nods. Sometimes we just held hands and looked into each other's eyes. There was no embarrassment for either of us as I helped remove her diaper. It was just another thing we did together, no different from me holding a slice of apple under her nose, or having a conversation, or quietly sitting at her bedside caressing her hand. After we finished cleaning her and putting on a new diaper, both of us gently moved her to a sitting position on the side of the bed. When changing her shirt, I stood next to her, gently supporting her back. Although we had completed everything, she refused to lie down and squeezed my hand.

"Do you want to sit up for a while?" I asked.

She nodded yes. I sat next to her on the bed, close enough so my entire arm supported her back.

"Is that okay?" I asked.

Yes, she nodded. As I held her, I felt her body against mine. While my left hand held hers, I gradually went from supporting to cradling, and I remembered the feelings I had when I held my daughter as an infant during a severe asthma attack. As the pain increased, so did the strength of her grip. Through her fingers I could experience her agony. At first, I thought she was just showing me that intense pain is bearable if it's shared. I felt as if she was saying, "I can't change what's happening to me, but I can learn to accept it with your support."

As I cradled her body with my right arm, her tension began to lessen. Then her grip changed, becoming soft and almost caressing. Occasionally, she released it and lovingly moved her fingers over mine. Gradually, I felt our roles shifting. I wasn't supporting her, she was comforting me. I realized it wasn't just a message about pain she was sending; it was also about letting go. I could live with my new condition as she did with hers, if I accepted support from people who had been offering it since the diagnosis. My family and friends were always ready to listen, but I was reluctant to open to them. In some ways Cindy was saying, "If I can be this revealing and dependent with you, can't you do the same with others?" She stayed in my arms for over thirty minutes, with me occasionally stroking her forehead and gently rocking her, as I once had done for my daughter when I couldn't do anything about her breathing.

Cindy gave me the first half of the lesson on letting go. The second half would come from Anna. When I was alone with Cindy I whispered the words, "It's okay to let go, Cindy." I hoped she could. "I know how much pain you're in. It's okay to start your journey."

She responded with a slow shake of her head.

"Your mother?" I asked. She nodded yes.

Although Cindy could accept the pain, she couldn't let go of her life as long as Anna wouldn't accept her death. As she closed her eyes, I kissed her on the forehead and tearfully left her room. I realized that acceptance wasn't always a solo performance. Anna's inability to accept Cindy's impending death was resulting in unimaginable pain for Cindy. It was probably one of the hardest things I ever witnessed in hospice—how the legitimate needs of one person can cause so much pain to someone they love. As a professional who spent his life "fixing" problems, I had to just watch and remain supportive of both. I began wondering how my unwillingness to accept my changing body was affecting my family and friends.

Three days later, I returned to the Guest House. After climbing the stairs to the second floor, I saw Anna standing outside Cindy's room. She looked different from the last time I'd seen her. She was walking, almost gracefully, toward me, her eyes dry and her facial muscles relaxed. We hugged as we usually did whenever I arrived or left.

Before I could say anything she said, "Last night I told Cindy how much I love her and will miss her."

Tears flowed as she smiled.

"I also told her it was all right to go."

It was the first time since Anna came to the House that I didn't hear an edginess in her voice, and it was the first time in many weeks—since I watched Cindy sniff the apple—that I felt joyful. As we approached Cindy's room, the sweet odor of the candles that had always been present in the hallway was barely detectable. When we entered the room I saw only a few lit candles. Anna gestured for me to sit by the side of the bed. Then she left us alone. Although alert, Cindy showed no recognition of me. The tension that had been present in her facial muscles was gone and her face was radiant. With eyes wide open, she occasionally made hand movements toward the end of her bed. She was smiling, and appeared to be having an animated conversation with someone I couldn't see.

As I wondered what it meant, another volunteer came into the room.

"Last night," she whispered to me, "Cindy began actively dying after Anna told her it was all right to go."

She left the room and allowed me to remain alone with Cindy. I sat with her and held her hand. When I saw other people standing outside the door waiting their turn for a private moment, I kissed her on the forehead, saying goodbye for what I knew was the last time.

"I'm going to miss you, Cindy. You've meant a lot to me. Thank you for what you've taught me. I love you. Have a good journey."

I don't know if she heard me. Although there was no sign she did, I had been told that people who are near death and appear unaware of their surroundings are often able to hear and understand. Two days later I received an e-mail from the hospice volunteer coordinator informing everyone that Cindy died peacefully that morning. A ceremonial bath was performed, and Cindy, "with a Mona Lisa" smile, was dressed in clothes Anna selected. The room was filled with flowers and candles, and Anna would sit vigil to welcome anyone who wished to say goodbye. The mortuary people would be there around 10:30 A.M., since Cindy wished to be picked up immediately. All were welcome to join in honoring her.

I immediately left for the hospice but arrived after the mortuary attendants were preparing to transport Cindy's body. Twelve people were at the bottom of the stairs waiting as Anna asked us to join her in singing Cindy's favorite childhood song, "You Are My Sunshine." I looked up and saw her body draped with a purple blanket on a stretcher and carried by two attendants. As they started down the stairs, Anna began singing. Volunteers and staff who knew the words joined in. Those who didn't hummed the melody as we all cried.

As the chorus ended, Cindy, covered with fresh flower petals, left the House.

For the next week, I asked myself if I had been holding on to parts of my life that no longer made sense, afraid of letting them go despite the pain it caused me and the anguish it brought to my family and friends. Between the hormone therapy and my fractured pelvis, I was no longer physically who I had been. At the core of this questioning was one very immediate dilemma: six months prior to Cindy's death I had agreed to go on a backcountry canoe trip in the Everglades with a friend. It was scheduled for two weeks after Cindy died. For five years, ever since my first canoe trip in the Everglades, I had cherished the spiritual nature of my solo journeys into the mangroves. It was a magical place in which I imagined life as it had been one hundred, five hundred, or even one thousand years ago. But along with the allure came built-in dangers, ranging from poisonous snakes to the occasional alligator, and with this trip I would experience one new challenge: the physical demands of the excursion itself. Should I go?

I decided not to cancel the trip. To do so meant that I was accepting my new limitations. Foolishly, I believed this could be a trip where I might resurrect a time when my body worked. My delusion painfully began unraveling as we loaded the canoe. If I was exhausted just carrying supplies fifty feet from the car, how would I be able to paddle for five days in the wilderness? As we pushed off from shore, my friend turned around and I saw a look of jubilation. Fortunately he turned forward before he could see my own expression, which I can only describe as reflecting an instant realization that I was making a terrible mistake. The canoe moved almost imperceptibly as we stroked our paddles in the brown waters of a strong incoming tide. I felt my arms strain and watched porpoises on both sides of the canoe effortlessly pass us.

I've come to believe that knowledge about life, even when given by gifted instructors, is rarely enough to effect lasting change in the way we actually live. The linguist Alfred Korzybski said it most elegantly, yet simply: "The map is not the territory." As I was struggling to do my share to prevent a crosswind from tipping over our canoe in snake-infested waters, my physical abilities didn't match my image of what I thought I should be able to do.

I was exhausted after fighting headwinds and the tide for six hours. We stopped for the night on a remote island, and I readied myself to fish. Fly-fishing had always been one of the activities I enjoyed most. As I waded out to a sandbar, I saw pods of fish waiting to be presented with a streamer. Moving forward, I sank up to my calves in clinging ooze that locked my feet, preventing me from going any farther. As I stood there out of casting range, I watched the tide take fish back into the welcoming Gulf. The mud released me only as I waded backward toward shore. There, I sat on a mound of broken shells, my rod limply in my hand and my unused flies at my side. I looked into the reflective waters, calm and timeless, and said to myself, "The map is not the territory."

Days later, unscathed except for the welts that covered our bodies from the bites of "no-see-um" flies, we returned with the incoming tide, the canoe gliding almost effortlessly toward the protected shore. As buildings slowly reappeared from behind the mangroves, I thought, *Maybe I'll come back next year—alone.*

I held on to this delusion for the next two weeks. That's when I was assigned to my first prostate cancer resident. Gus was an internationally known journalist whose cancer had metastasized to his bones. He was heavily medicated to relieve his intense pain. I had read in the research literature that if my cancer couldn't be controlled, it would invade my bones, and so I knew that in the future I might suffer as Gus did. He was asleep when I arrived, and the attendant believed he wouldn't wake for my entire shift.

Sometimes being a bedside volunteer involves just sitting with a patient, often for hours. During those times I held their hand, read, reflected on what I was experiencing, or wrote. That night I brought a book containing poems by Mizuta Masahide, a sixteenth-century samurai. When he returned home from one of his many diplomatic missions for the emperor, he found his house destroyed by a fire. It became the basis of his most famous haiku:

Barn's burnt down—
now
I can see the moon*

My barn began burning with the diagnosis. What would I see when it was gone? What was Cindy trying to tell me? What were the Everglades screaming into my ears? And what did Gus and Masahide conspire to drum into my thick skull? They were all saying that life moves on whether you want it to or not. If you hold on to the past, grasping onto what no longer exists, you'll create havoc for yourself and others. But if you let go, a whole new world is right there—no longer hidden by your memories.

* From *Zen Poetry: Let the Spring Breeze Enter,* edited and translated by Lucien Stryk and Takashi Ikemoto (New York: Grove Press, 1977).

3

Unconditional Giving

> Giving is more joyous than receiving, not because it is a deprivation, but because in the act of giving lies the expression of my aliveness.
>
> —Erich Fromm

In many ways, my life before the cancer was like a series of minicontracts. If I did *x* then I'd expect *y* to occur. If I put myself out for someone, then I'd expect him or her to do the same when I needed help. I never consciously created such contracts, but now I realize that in many ways I was relating with the people in my life with unexpressed expectations. For me, all parties were obligated to perform, to reciprocate. When people didn't meet my expectations, I indiscriminately began applying the word "ungrateful." It became even more frequent when the cancer treatment began.

Looking back at my life as it was then, I see that it parodied the story of the rich man who laid a bag of gold at the feet of a monastery's abbot. When the abbot ignored him and continued weeding his garden, the rich man asked the abbot why he hadn't acknowledged his great generosity. The abbot asked why the man gave the gold. "Because it is my way of pleasing God," he said. The abbot responded that if it was a business transaction, he'd get a piece of paper and sign a thank-you note from God. That way the rich man would have something that stated he did a meritorious act for Judgment Day. But if he was giving the gold from his heart, why did he need a thank you? With that, the man left. When I met Sid in hospice, I realized I was no different from the rich man.

Before every shift change, the volunteers finishing and those beginning would meet with a staff member to discuss what was happening with the residents. It was also a time to share feelings about how our involvement was changing us. When it was my turn to speak, I used the same words I had been using since I began my hospice service: "It's been an interesting and incredibly enlightening week."

But I paused that day and added, "But I hope this week won't be." Everyone looked at me, wondering what I meant. I explained that since I had been there I had learned more about myself than I had during the past fifty-eight years of my life. I needed a break to digest all the changes.

Everyone laughed at that. Although it was taken as a joke, I wasn't kidding. For six months I had been involved in the lives of dozens of people whom I fed, cleaned, and grew to love. But with each encounter my understanding of life was changed. Just when I thought I understood the importance of something like "forgiveness" or "compassion," the concepts became refined or were stood on their head by a simple interaction. For example, I thought I understood "gratitude" until a very proper professor asked me to empty his overflowing urinal. "Someone of your educational stature shouldn't have to do this," he said. Until he died two weeks later, he would thank me on every visit for that simple act of kindness. Expressing gratitude, he said, meant that he was helpless to do those things that had been routine, those simple things that are a part of living. Meanwhile, I began applying the lessons I was learning in my personal life. Just when my family and friends were getting used to one Stan, a softer one replaced him. Although the changes were positive—for instance, now I was more grateful for anything that was done for me—the unexpected changes were becoming emotionally exhausting for them.

On this particular Tuesday, when I met Sid, I thought we had only one resident in the House that night, since two had died the previous week, and as far as I knew, nobody else had been admitted. It had been a difficult month for me, both physically and psychologically. Going up and down the stairs all the time was delaying the healing process of my pelvis fracture. And, in addition to my regular shift, I was spending at least one overnight a week with a resident.

"It should be a quiet night," one of the volunteers said. "Sid, our new resident, is sleeping. He's a wonderful person. I spent time with him and his family earlier today. He has hepatitis C and cirrhosis, so don't be shocked when you see his yellow color."

We all understood the warning about hepatitis C. With a little common sense and awareness, care for these patients was no different from serving a patient with a noninfectious illness. When the meeting was over I went upstairs and looked into Sid's room. The lights were out and he was sleeping. I returned downstairs to clean the kitchen and finish the laundry.

At 8:30 I thought of going home early. Everything was done, Sid was sleeping, and Dorothy, another volunteer, was sitting with a resident. I was about to go back upstairs to ask her if she would mind if I left early, but I decided to make myself a cup of coffee and just sit alone in the kitchen for a little while. As I sat and waited for the coffee to brew, staying a little while longer at the House seemed to be the right thing to do.

Since the diagnosis, I had been faced with a series of decisions, each one of which would lead me on a different path. Should I retire or keep teaching? Retiring would give me time to enjoy my passions for music and fishing, but would I like giving up the status of being a university professor? Should we move to the North Bay or stay in San Francisco? The North Bay would be peaceful, but I would lose the excitement of the city. Should I focus my writing on easily published material or concentrate on substantive issues with a reduced possibility of being published? "Fluff" pieces would give me more print potential, but what difference would they make in people's lives? Should I volunteer for hospice or start an intensive physical training program? The first would promote the comfort of others, the second my physical recovery. Hardly a month went by when I didn't have to make a lifestyle-altering decision. For someone who had sought stability throughout his entire life, this difficulty in making decisions was upsetting. But somehow, in retrospect, I had mostly been making the right decisions—and for some intriguing reason, I always felt I was getting help from an unknown source.

As I sat there with my coffee, I thought about the remarkable experiences I had been having, and I was thankful to be going home early without having to assimilate another one this week. I remembered one of the Monty Python sketches in the movie *The Meaning of Life,* where a man is stuffing himself with whatever food is placed in front of him. As his gluttony increases, so does the size of his body. It overflows his chair. As he lies back covered with the food he couldn't fit into his mouth, the maitre d' asks him if he would like a mint. Groaning from all the food, he declines, only consenting after the maitre d' explains that the mint is "wafer-thin." When the diner agrees and begins savoring the mint, he literally explodes over the entire room. I felt the same could happen to me. One more life lesson, even a little one, and I'd explode.

"Stan," Dorothy called from the second floor. "Martha needs you to help with Sid."

Maybe this would be simple, just a soiled-linen change and then back downstairs or home. The crystal chandelier in Sid's room was fully illuminated. He was a big man, maybe 250 pounds, although it was hard to tell with his swollen belly. And, just as described, he was a dull shade of yellow.

As I pulled on the latex gloves from my back pocket, I wondered if he felt it was another barrier between him and the "healthy" world. I knew I was probably generalizing from my own "latex glove" experiences, but in some ways, I envisioned myself as similar to Sid, even though I knew nothing about him. When the term "cancer" was used to label me, I became a different person in the eyes of many in the "healthy" world. Being labeled reduced me to an illness. I was no longer a full university professor, husband, father, writer, or any of the other words I had previously used to describe myself. I became a medical label that caused the complexity of my identity to evaporate. And most frightening was, eventually I bought into it—I became my label. I allowed the term "cancer survivor" to separate me from the healthy world just as effectively as my latex gloves separated me from Sid.

"Hi, Sid. I'm Stan. I'm a volunteer and I'll be helping Martha change you."

In a soft voice, Sid said, "Thank you."

He was six feet seven inches tall, he had acute hepatitis C, he was transferred only hours earlier from a hospital intensive care unit, and he was aware he was dying. Yet, his voice sounded more like someone sharing intimacies with a loved one than a person in intense pain. As we carefully turned him from his back to his side, his peaceful expression changed to one that tried to hide the intense pain I knew he was experiencing. After we had him balanced on his side, Martha realized that some of the supplies necessary for changing him were downstairs.

"I have to find some pads before we can start." Then turning to Sid, she said, "I'm sorry. We can either have you return to lying on your back, or Stan can continue holding you on your side."

"It's fine the way I am," he said without any hesitation.

Watching his body quiver and looking at his face, I knew it wasn't fine. But probably the pain he was experiencing was less than what he would have felt if we moved him again. Martha left to get more pads, and I heard her footsteps almost at a running gait going down the stairs.

"Are you having any pain?" I asked. "I know this is an uncomfortable position I'm holding you in."

"Just a little," he said, almost apologizing.

"Would you like me to try to coach you through your discomfort?" I said to Sid.

Although I'd never led any breathing or relaxation exercises before, I had been meditating for years and after my operation I used a series of breathing exercises to lessen the pain. And why I made the suggestion, I didn't know. But he said he'd like to try.

"As you breathe in, imagine an intense white light coming into your body and going directly to the parts that hurt. As you exhale, envision a black cloud coming out containing all the pain."

By the time Martha returned, we had been doing the exercise for ten minutes. Sid's body was considerably less tense and he was no longer quivering. We continued the exercise throughout the changing process. When everything was done and we repositioned him, he smiled and looked up at us through yellow eyes.

"Thank you," he said as Martha left the room.

"I know that tired you out," I said. "Would you like me to leave or stay and sit with you for a while?"

"No, please stay. I'd appreciate that."

I pulled up a chair and sat next to him so that we were close to being at the same eye level. It was one of the first things I learned in my hospice training. There were so many barriers between someone who was dying and those who weren't, something as simple as just sitting across from the person, rather than looking down at them, made a difference. I decided to wait until he took the initiative to speak. And if he didn't, I was prepared to just sit until he fell asleep and then leave. I hadn't even settled into the chair when Sid began speaking.

"Before I came here I was in the IC unit. I watched a team of doctors and nurses around me. Everyone was talking and working furiously. I knew I was in trouble, but could only watch. Then, from behind all of those doctors, I saw someone who shouldn't have been there."

"A doctor?" I asked.

"I don't think so. I didn't recognize him. He was just standing there watching, and that smile, that beautiful smile was incredible. I still remember the feeling it gave me, but his features were a blur. Then he was gone and I don't remember anything until I woke and saw a nurse standing over me. When she said they almost lost me, I told her I knew. I thought she was about to lecture me on the effects of anesthesia, so I described everything I remembered. Judging by the look on her face, I must have been accurate right down to the instruments they were using and the doctor's curses when he thought I died. When I asked about the man standing behind everyone, she said, 'There was no one else in the room.'"

"Another patient I've met had a similar experience," I said. I told him about Bill, who when completely awake, saw his wife standing at the end of the bed.

"What do you think it means?" he asked.

"I don't know."

"Guess."

"Well, from what I've observed and read, people who are nearing death often see people they know, who, I'm told, beckon them to come."

"To where?"

"I don't know. Those people I've spoken to who've had the experience say the person was welcoming them."

"Did they die shortly after seeing the person?"

"No. Bill died two weeks later."

Bill had spent almost a half-hour describing it to me, emphasizing that he wasn't crazy and he didn't think it was "random firings" of his neurons, as scientists had described that type of thing in the many books he had read. For Bill, who had no religious or spiritual beliefs, the presence of his wife was just as real as the conversation he was having with me.

"Sid, you didn't have any dinner. Can I get you something?"

"They said I can have ice cream."

"What kind would you like?"

"Anything plain would be cool," he said, smiling when he realized he'd just made an unintended pun.

"Vanilla?"

"That'd be great."

As I walked down the stairs to the kitchen, I kept hearing the question, "Would you like just one wafer-thin mint?"

As I scooped the ice cream into the bowl, memories of Jim came back to me; I remembered him savoring each spoonful I fed him as if it was a soufflé made with expensive Belgian chocolate.

"If you'd like, I can feed it to you," I offered as I reentered the room with the bowl of ice cream.

"No, that's okay. If you just raise the bed I can do it myself." He put the first spoonful of ice cream into his mouth with a quivering hand. "Oh!" he said loudly as his head went back and his eyes closed. *My God, I killed him!* I jumped out of my chair and hovered over him.

"Sid? Sid?"

Slowly exhaling, he opened his eyes and said, "I'm fine. That was marvelous. This is so good."

I don't know what it is about ice cream, but Sid's was the same reaction Jim and three other residents had. Maybe it's an allegory for moving toward death. Going from something solid that's definable, then into a liquid form, and finally disappearing, leaving only lasting memories. Most likely it's just something incredibly refreshing and tasty to someone who is very sick. As Sid savored the ice cream we spoke about our lives and were surprised several times by how similar our histories were. During the 1960s we both were involved in the civil rights movement. He stayed in Boston to organize and protest; I went south for the Selma-to-Montgomery march. Our parents could not understand why their nice, college-educated, Jewish boy would do something like that. We both had had the chance to meet leaders we admired: he met some of the Kennedys during a protest in Boston; I had a private meeting with Martin Luther King Jr. in Montgomery. Both of us had been arrested; he had spent a day in jail, and I had spent a week in jail on a hunger strike. Both of us had gone through rocky times in our marriages, although mine ended fortunately, in reconciliation. His marriage had ended in divorce. Our lives were running on parallel courses, just a few degrees apart. Sometimes they almost merged, as when we both thought about attending the same spiritual retreat but decided at the last minute not to. When there was a lull in the conversation, I looked at him and wondered if the direction of our lives would still continue in unison. We talked for what seemed like hours. But I don't think it was more than forty-five minutes.

"You know, I've been sick for only a few weeks. I'm on a liver transplant list; but I know there's not enough time. And even if there is, I'm too sick for it to be successful. I'm going to die soon and it's okay. I look at death as just another step to something else," he continued.

"I understand. I started realizing I was on some sort of journey about a year ago."

"What happened?"

"It started with prostate cancer and a visit to Laguna Honda Hospital.

"Isn't that the other place Zen Hospice serves?"

"Yes. At a party someone asked me if I would visit his partner in the hospice ward. He knew I was a speech-language pathologist and hoped that I could help the staff communicate with his partner who had a stroke. I visited and was overwhelmed by what I saw."

"The people who were dying?"

"No. It was a few people who were wearing ordinary street clothes and gliding between the patients who impressed me so deeply. They moved differently from the staff, who all seemed to be late for an appointment. It seemed to me that when they looked at a patient, their eyes didn't slide away to anything or anyone else. It seemed that in that moment only the patient existed for them."

"Who were they?"

"Volunteers. I saw peacefulness in their faces, the likes of which I never saw. I knew that whatever was creating that expression had something to do with what they were doing right at that moment. And whatever that was, I wanted to experience it."

"Did you?"

"Yes, I do now, every day I come here. I feel it's another step on some type of journey I'm on. Once I arrived here, I thought the steps would end. But they didn't."

"And my bedside?" he said, smiling. "Is this another step?"

"I'm sure of it. I could have left before you woke, but I lingered over a cup of coffee this evening."

"Do you think this is your final destination? Being here at the hospice?"

"I don't think so. It doesn't feel like it."

"Where do you think it will take you?"

"I've been asking myself that same question for months. Where the hell am I going and who or what is leading me there?" We both laughed. I took a long breath and finally said what had been on my mind for months. "I've come to believe there aren't any coincidences in my life."

"Yes, I know what you mean. I feel the same way."

"For the last two years I've been coming to crossroads," I said. "I can choose to go one way or another. As I look back, I believe I've generally made good decisions. But how that happened, I have no idea. At times I think someone or something is behind me, gently nudging me in a certain direction, like my mother would do when I was a child."

He nodded his head in agreement. "That's the same with me. Do you ever look back and wonder how you were able to do some of the things you did?" I thought he might be referring to the civil rights movement.

"Yes," I said. I thought about the many things I was able to do with the residents that would have been unthinkable for me only months before. Sid was exhausted, but I knew he wouldn't stop the conversation until I ended it. For both of us, it was like indulging in a rich food neither of us wanted to finish.

"Sid, you're exhausted," I said reluctantly. "I think it may be time for you to rest."

"Yes, I think you're right. I am tired. Could you bring over my pillows?"

When Martha and I changed him, we had removed all the pillows, blankets, and a small white stuffed rhinoceros. Only the blanket and pillow for his head had been replaced. I think he may have been embarrassed to ask for a child's toy after having a conversation about his life and his coming death.

After placing the pillows on both sides of the bed, I handed him the rhinoceros.

"Thanks," he said. He lay back on his pillow for a short while, then opened his eyes and looked at me as I was getting ready to leave.

"I'll see you again when I bring in those tapes," I said.

Earlier, we had talked about a set of audiotapes of a workshop on death and dying I had recorded. When he asked to hear them, I said I'd bring them in on Saturday, even though my shift wasn't until the following Thursday. I realized I'd been given a rare opportunity to be with a very special person—a sweet and gentle giant who was able to gracefully accept his own death. This grace was something I wanted to emulate when it was my turn.

"There's only one thing I regret about dying early," he said.

"What's that?"

Gesturing to a picture next to his bed he said, "I won't have the opportunity to see my son become an adult."

"How old is he?"

"Eighteen."

"My guess is you've taught him your values."

"Yes."

"Will they guide him into being the person you'd like him to be?"

He thought for a minute, then smiled. "He already is."

As I walked out of his room I knew Sid's death was going to affect me more than anyone else's had so far. In one hour, I felt I had a new close friend. I wanted to spend as much time as I could with him, but there was a protocol at the Guest

House; social visits from volunteers to residents during non-shift hours weren't encouraged. Our role was not that of a friend or family member. As volunteers, we were there to provide comfort, compassion, and to help patients die with dignity. Nonetheless, I also wanted to be Sid's friend. When I came to deliver the promised tapes on Saturday, I saw that he had deteriorated substantially. I was disappointed when I saw another volunteer with him having what seemed like a serious conversation. I quickly handed the volunteer the tapes and prepared to leave.

"Stan, thank you. Thanks for everything," Sid said in a barely audible voice.

I had been thanked by residents in the past. Some residents thanked the volunteers on an hourly basis. Sometimes when residents said thank you, I could hear their gratitude in their tone. At other times it was in their words. But in Sid's simple "thank you," I could hear a finality that broke my heart. On Monday, all the volunteers received an e-mail telling us that Sid had died early that morning. It described how throughout the night he had kept his eyes open and looked at the attendant. Then shortly before he died, he looked skyward and reached his arm up in a slight wave. The e-mail concluded, "Everyone is welcome to sit with Sid until his body is removed later in the day." I arrived at 7:00 A.M., hoping I would have time alone with him. At that hour only the attendant and I were in the House. The first shift of volunteers wasn't scheduled to arrive until 9:00 A.M.

I sat down next to Sid and saw the rhinoceros was still nestled between his arm and his body, and the picture of his son had been moved to a rolling tray directly in front of him. I realized that I felt a little cheated. I would have liked more time with him. He was the type of person I could share a drink with. Someone I would look forward to spending time with. In short, he would have been a good buddy, and I felt angry that he was taken away.

Instead of giving him my compassion as a hospice volunteer without any expectation of receiving, I found myself demanding something of him—his friendship. Sitting alone next to him, I realized that giving with an expectation of receiving something—anything—defeated the whole purpose of being compassionate. If I gave something, and truly felt it was the right thing to do, then why was it necessary to get anything in return?

Before the cancer, I had a friend in San Francisco with whom I spent a lot of time. For the most part, we had the same values, and both of us grew up on the East Coast. During the months when he and his wife were divorcing, I would spend hours with him every day, consoling, advising, or just listening. Later, when I was facing a financial crisis, I asked for his help in inflating the value of an object that had been stolen and was covered by my insurance. When he refused, I was furious. If I could spend months listening to his problems, sometimes for three or four continuous hours, then shouldn't he have felt obligated to help me? After Sid died, however, I contacted this old friend and apologized for my dishonorable behavior—for asking him for something that ethically he was not able to do. Three years had passed since we had spoken, and he was stunned to hear from me with my admittance that I was wrong. Although he accepted my apology, our relationship was never rekindled. During our conversation I realized I caused him such incredible pain, he still hadn't recovered from it. And it was needless. Although our friendship wasn't based on a business contract, my insistence in acting as if we had a contract destroyed the relationship.

I didn't spiritually "burst" when I was sitting with Sid after his death. In hospice, there is always a little more room for new insights, no matter how full we feel, and the most affecting insights always seemed to occur for me when I sat quietly alone with someone after they died. Their presence produced a certain clarity of thought for me—or maybe clarity of heart—that's difficult to describe. In some traditions, bodies are left untouched for up to three days after a death, in the belief that it takes that long for the soul to move on. Maybe my heart was picking up Sid's presence as his consciousness departed or his soul ascended, filling me with gems of wisdom—his final gift. As I heard the front door opening, I kissed him on the forehead and left, thankful for deciding to accept the "wafer-thin" mint.

4

Heart Communication

> We shouldn't believe that talking is the
> only way to communicate; talking may be
> an obstacle to communication.
>
> —Thich Nhat Hanh

I was a speech-language pathologist for more than thirty years, and it was my job to help people become more proficient at using words. Under my tutelage, they would become "facile" with language, eventually developing into more proficient speakers who could express any thought or feeling. If their language wasn't fully developed, I taught them new linguistic structures. If their speech was too flowery or imprecise, I showed them how to simplify it. When their thoughts lost a logical progression, I drew a map they could follow. I believed that only through words could communication be true and important. As I reflect back on my life, I wonder if my choice of this profession had something to do with a fear of communicating from the heart. Was I searching for a nonthreatening way of doing that? If I was, I didn't find it until the cancer was discovered.

By "heart communication" I mean the expressions of

feelings and emotions—minimizing analytical rigor and maximizing unadorned honesty. In the past I felt heart communications were fine for those intimate moments when I wasn't vulnerable or didn't care what people thought. Unfortunately, that applied only to a minuscule number of my daily interactions. I used heart communication always with my dogs, usually with my family, sometimes with friends, rarely with acquaintances, and never with strangers. In general, I found the expression of emotions to be just too messy. Even when my cancer was diagnosed, I avoided dealing with my feelings. I had a month between the diagnosis and the operation. One month to accept the possibility that even if I made the right choice, I might become an asexual person with no bladder control. For me, at that time, the first outcome meant a loss of masculinity; the second, a loss of dignity. Instead of asking myself how I would deal with each possibility with Wendy, I chose to pose questions to myself as if I were preparing a lecture for professionals at a conference. *What would be the various consequences if the cancer wasn't contained? What would be the logistics of incontinence? What are the adverse psychological effects of impotency? Could the outcomes be rank-ordered by acceptability? Was a little incontinence better than a little impotence? Was it better to die soon or live incontinent and impotent?* For each question, I typed at least two answers, with a multitude of cross-references and research citations. Very scientific. Very delusional.

Wendy asked me if I wanted to talk about my cancer, but I brushed her off, insisting that I didn't need to discuss it; I was calm and ready for anything. *Right! I was about to have major surgery that could radically change or end my life and I was calm?* I knew she wasn't buying it. But given our history—she wanted to talk about feelings and I wanted to run from them—she didn't pursue it. When Wendy asked again a week before the operation if I was ready to talk, I wanted to say yes, but I couldn't. Instead, I shook my head no. If I talked about it, I wouldn't be able to hide my fear of what I might become. I felt as if I were a contestant on *Let's Make a Deal*. Which door do I choose? Behind one was a diaper, a eunuch was behind another, and the grim reaper lurked behind door number three. It would have been nice to have a fourth door.

At 4:30 A.M. on the day of my surgery, I drove to the hospital with Wendy as my passenger. We had been together for over thirty years, and yet she still felt guarded discussing her feelings with me. I looked at her and wondered why she had stayed with me so long. Every night since the diagnosis, I knew, she had been confiding in our daughter, Jessica. But I was keeping everyone at a distance, redirecting their concerns away from me. My children had flown in to give me support, and I acted as if it was just a pleasant holiday visit.

One hour before surgery, I sat in a recliner in a surgery-prep room with nondescript pastel walls. In the corner was a loudspeaker over which elevator music was playing at a volume so low I couldn't identify the melody. It seemed that someone thought that by making an artificially calm environment, the calm would magically be absorbed into the minds of people who were sitting there waiting for their operations, wondering if there would be a tomorrow. The only thing that felt real to me was the intent look on Wendy's face.

"Don't worry, you're not getting rid of me this easily," I said. "I'll be around for a long time."

She wasn't amused. And she didn't know, I found out later, how to comfort me because I appeared to be facing this major operation as if I were waiting for the mechanic to fix my car. I looked at a book I brought from home as a technician came into the room rolling a cart that looked to me like equipment from the torture chambers of the Spanish Inquisition. In it were instruments to pick, poke, cuff, and shave me. There were also little vials—some already filled with blood, others waiting for mine. After completing all her tasks, the technician left the room smiling and motioned to a nurse.

"Can you imagine?" I heard her whispering. "He'll be on the table soon and look how calm he is." The nurse nodded, and I thought I heard her say, "Maybe the new colors and music are working."

No one had noticed that I wasn't turning the pages of my book; I didn't have any idea what I was looking at. I don't know if by pretending to read I was trying to calm myself or reduce Wendy's anxiety. When Jessica and my son, Justin, entered the pre-op area, I heard a nurse ask them if they would like to see their father before he went into surgery. Her tone was reminiscent of the one my mother's surgeon used when he explained to me she might not survive her operation. Both tearfully came into the room, trying to smile.

"It's all right. I know you're worried, but I'll be fine," I said as I looked beyond them at the wall clock. It was 7:50, and surgery was scheduled for 8:00. After my children kissed me, they quietly stood in a corner of the room. I focused on controlling my smile and the tone of my voice. I had often done the same thing in therapy when a client revealed something shocking, or if I was bored. I had always thought it was important in counseling to present a neutral demeanor—one that was non-reactive. I lost my poker face with the entry of the hospital social worker. She was wearing a brightly colored shirt with a bow that brought back memories of a television clown I remembered as a young child. He would bounce around on the black and white screen doing ridiculous things, impervious to the chaos he was creating. The social worker had come to discuss a document they forgot to give me a week before at the presurgery conference.

"I'd like you to look at this advance directive," she said. "So if something should go wrong during the operation, and I'm sure it won't, we'll know what to do."

Behind her back, my family winced, the harsh fluorescent lights exaggerating their pained expressions. I looked at the page and saw it listed every problem that could occur: septic shock, aneurisms, uncontrolled bleeding, incontinence, impotence, severe brain damage, and of course, death. As if the words weren't frightening enough, they were written in italics. At the end of the document it asked if they should try heroic efforts to save my vegetative life if someone screwed up during the operation. Oh, and if there was a dispute about the operation's outcome, would I go to arbitration rather than using lawyers? These were the same types of objective words I had relied on throughout my life for comfort. But they were not comforting on that day. In ten seconds, one piece of paper listing everything that could go wrong shattered a protective barrier from reality that I had been carefully nurturing for a month. Barely able to grip the pen, I signed it, and again wondered which door I would wake up behind. Waiting outside the room was a nurse in surgery scrubs who entered when the social worker left.

"It's time," she said, as if telling a young child to prepare for school. It was exactly eight o'clock when I kissed Wendy, Jessica, and Justin, and walked toward the operating room with the nurse.

That moment marked the end of my ability to force the world to fit into neat categories; from then on, my life became "messy." Although I would emerge from surgery without becoming incontinent or impotent, I would still have to deal with the presence in my body of runaway cancer cells. "Certainty" was gone in my life. And with that, the very foundation of my relationships with the world had changed. Communication through words—something I had relied upon my entire professional life—proved to be inadequate for expressing how I felt about my situation and what I wanted to communicate to the people I served.

The feeling I had about my life and my hospice experiences required me to go beyond the precision of my beloved words. I learned through these experiences the value of communicating feelings through touch, ritual, breath, actions, and music.

Six months after my operation I entered Alisa's room at the Guest House with two plates of food. She was a large woman with a disarming smile that was always there when the pain wasn't too intense. She was lying in bed with her granddaughter snuggled next to her.

"I've made nan, dal, raita, Bombay potatoes, and curried chicken salad."

"How nice that you made Indian food for us," Alisa said.

For two weeks she and her husband, Norman, had patiently accepted the excellent but bland food prepared for them. Since coming to the United States more than twenty years ago, Alisa had devoted her life to perfecting the gourmet preparation of her native Indian food. What they considered "spicy" was outrageously hot to everyone else. What was spicy to everyone in the hospice was tasteless to them. Norman sat in the corner of the room with that look of sleep deprivation I was all too familiar with, having lived with a sleep disorder for seven years.

"You've outdone yourself," Alisa said, smiling. "Thank you so much. I'll eat mine later."

I placed both plates on a dresser and sat down by the side of the bed. Norman looked up from the newspaper I didn't think he was reading and thanked me. He would wait to eat with Alisa. Her granddaughter was lying on Alisa's left side—the side that was paralyzed when her cancer metastasized to her brain, causing a series of strokes.

"She's beautiful," I said looking at her granddaughter.

"Thank you. Her name's Alba. Alba, say hello to Stan."

Her granddaughter looked like a baby bird completely engulfed by its protective mother. Alisa could feel the child's tiny three-year-old body but couldn't move her arm to hold or caress her. Alba hid her face in the pillow until Alisa convinced her to come out by gently nudging her with her chin.

"Hi," she said softly while smiling at me.

After kissing her grandmother goodnight, Alba slid off the bed and went downstairs to join her mother. They would return every day while Alisa lived. Norman rarely left the hospice, spending every night on a mattress on the floor next to his wife's bed. I left and went downstairs to the kitchen. When I was washing the dishes, Norman came in with his empty plate and his wife's full one.

"I'm sorry she didn't eat anything. She wasn't feeling well today. But as you can see, I ate everything. It was very good."

It really wasn't, but he and Alisa seemed to appreciate my effort, regardless of the outcome.

"I'm glad you liked it."

He looked at me for a while, and then took a deep breath. "You know she wants to die at home."

"Where's that?"

"Las Vegas. But that's not possible. There's no way we can get her back there. And even if we can, I can't take care of her by myself. And there isn't any place like this where we live."

"Is there anything more we can do to make her stay here easier?"

"No. Everyone is so kind. I've never seen a place like this. She just wants to be home. She wants to die in her own bed." It was something I heard from most people, whether they came from the wealthy suburbs of San Francisco or lived in the transient hotels of the Tenderloin.

Norman and I talked about the deplorable care Alisa received at a facility here in the Bay Area following her stroke.

He was upset because he wasn't able to be more effective in getting her better care. Before retiring, he had owned a company in India, where his orders were unquestioningly followed. But since he had been trying to get services for his wife six hundred miles away from home, he felt helpless.

"We've been married for forty years, and she still treats me as if we're newlyweds." Then he paused before softly saying, "I don't know what I'll do without her."

In the past, I would have tried using consoling words. It was a constant battle to remember that there were things I couldn't fix.

"You know Alisa likes to have her arm and foot massaged?" Norman said.

"Yes." I knew the pain she felt in her arm and leg was constant.

"She looks forward to it every day." I didn't respond. "There always seems to be someone here who can give very good massages," he said, still waiting for me to say something.

I knew Norman was hoping I would offer a massage. But I had been told by someone with bone cancer that my massage skills were poor. "Stop!" he had yelled. "It hurts now more than when you started."

That was the last time I offered a massage to anyone, despite knowing that some people desperately wanted and needed one. When anyone asked, I went to find another volunteer who was more experienced than I was. If I couldn't find someone, I invented a reason for not doing it. There was always some plumbing or electrical problem that needed my immediate attention.

"Why don't we find Louise?" I said. "Her massages are incredible."

When we went upstairs, I realized Louise was with another resident and probably would remain with him for the remainder of the shift. Norman walked into Alisa's room and from the hallway I heard, "Stan is here to give you a massage." I sheepishly entered.

"Oh, thank you," Alisa said. "I would appreciate it so much. It makes the pain go away."

I was concerned about again hurting someone with my ineptitude. Unlike the first person I massaged, Alisa might be too gracious to tell me if I was hurting her. Her expression seemed to show that she expected relief.

"If I do anything that hurts, please tell me. I won't know unless you do."

"Don't worry Stan, I'm sure it will be fine," she said with the tone and type of smile you see on a mother's face as she tries to encourage her child to do something frightening.

During one training session, a massage therapist suggested that when we do massage, we should try to remember how we stroke our pets. There is a way we convey love to our animals that is neither learned nor contrived. It's as if we don't need to worry what anyone thinks of us as we display affection. When we stroke our pets, the only thing we're doing is showing them love. We have no hidden agendas or images we're trying to protect.

I've always lived with dogs, and even though I understood immediately what the therapist was saying, emotional honesty with an animal was different from emotional honesty with a human being. There is no threat in being open with an animal. If they don't accept what you're offering, they don't make you feel bad, or hold it against you, or tell all of their friends what a fool you made of yourself. Until that day with Alisa, I viewed the therapist's suggestion as "an interesting idea" but not something I could allow myself to do.

I fought my fear and focused on using touch to convey the love I felt for Alisa.

"Ah, that feels so nice," she said as I hesitantly massaged her arm.

I finally relaxed, and we continued: Alisa, in a dreamlike state; me, astonished that I was providing comfort.

"That's so wonderful. Would you mind if I close my eyes and just experience it?"

"No, please do," I said. For the next twenty minutes, with Norman sitting in a chair in the corner looking content, and the odors of my Indian food still lingering in the air, I gently massaged her foot until she fell asleep.

The thought came to me, as I finished my shift that night, that massage for the dying was not about knowing how to give the perfect massage but rather it was about establishing a connection with another human being. With Alisa's encouragement and assurances, my hands had been capable of expressing feelings I never thought possible; the commonality I felt with a dying person, an understanding of what they were experiencing, and my willingness to be present during fear and pain. I had expected a disaster, but instead, I realized, I had just experienced one of the most communicative moments of my life—without the use of a single word.

I realized, too, that in my own life I had been figuratively refusing to allow myself to be touched by anyone. Family and friends had extended their hands to me since the diagnosis, but I continually rejected their comfort. I felt that if I accepted help, it meant that I was ready to give up being an independent and physically intact person.

I had been doing evening shifts for months. I preferred them, because it was during the quiet evening hours that residents often wanted to talk about their lives. It was these discussions that were changing and enriching my life. But the hormone injections that were part of my cancer treatment had been playing havoc with my already bizarre sleep patterns and varying energy levels. Reluctantly, as I left Alisa that night, I decided to change my shift to the morning, which would be easier on my body. Looking back now, I realize it was the first step in accepting my reduced abilities.

One evening soon after I began my new schedule, I arrived at the House for a training session where I would be giving new volunteers a presentation on what I had learned in hospice. I brought food for the session, and as I dropped off everything in the kitchen, I was feeling somewhat distracted. I wanted to check in with Alisa, who had been sleeping when I left after my morning shift earlier in the day. But I was also thinking about what I would say to the new volunteers this evening, and in addition I was preoccupied with a lecture I would be presenting in North Carolina in just a couple of days. I turned to Mike, another volunteer, who was preparing food.

"Mike, please tell Jennifer I'll be at the meeting after I

visit with Alisa. I didn't have a chance to say goodbye this morning."

I started walking up the stairs but Mike was following me.

"Stan," he said in a soft voice, "You probably don't know, but she's beginning to go."

Earlier during my shift that morning, Alisa had appeared weaker but not actively dying. When I entered her room, the attendant was at her side and Norman was pacing at the other end of the room.

"She's not doing well," he said.

The attendant nodded in agreement while gently stroking Alisa's forehead with one hand and feeling her pulse with the other. Her breathing was shallow, and gaps had developed between breaths. It probably would be only days. Family members were on the way, and those who feared they'd be too late were calling to say goodbye. One call came as I was sitting at her side.

"It's Dave," a volunteer said, handing the phone to Norman.

Dave, Alisa's oldest son, had visited the prior week, but had to return to the East Coast.

"Alisa," Norman said in a loud voice. "It's Dave." He held the phone to her ear.

She opened her eyes and in a barely audible voice kept repeating, "Yes, I love you too, I love you too." I remembered these were also the last words my mother and I said to each other before she died. When Alisa was no longer able to speak, Norman took the phone and continued the conversation outside the room.

"Stan, can you stay with Alisa until I come back?" the attendant asked. "I have to give medicine to another resident."

"Of course."

Alone in the room with her, I gently held Alisa's hand. After a few minutes I realized that I was massaging her arm, just as I had done on my evening shift not long ago. She opened her eyes and smiled as she looked in my direction.

"Stan," she said, almost in a whisper.

"Hi, Alisa. When I left this morning you were asleep and I didn't have a chance to say goodbye."

In the past when I'd say goodbye at the end of my shift, we kissed, and she'd embrace me with her right arm when she had the energy. I'd be saying more than our usual goodbye today, because I was going out of town.

"You've meant very much to me," I said. "Your love has filled my heart. I'll miss you, but I know you'll soon begin your journey."

"Yes," she said, with tears pooling in the corners of her eyes. "Will it be hard?"

"I don't know, but with all the love in your heart, I don't think so."

"I'm not so sure."

"Just let go when you're ready and think of those things that brought you joy."

"But there are the bad memories too."

I didn't know what those were, and I was not about to ask. "Think of your granddaughter and the good things you've done in your life."

She smiled and nodded before losing consciousness. Again

the breathing became shallow, and there were longer gaps between breaths. I went downstairs to do my presentation, answering questions on automatic pilot, frequently glancing toward the stairs that led to Alisa's room. As I left, thoughts of her came up in my mind: a conversation about our passion for coffee, her love for her granddaughter, and her gracious attempt to eat the terrible home-cooked Indian dinner I had made. But the one memory that I knew would last the longest was the massage I had given her. The way she helped me to gain some confidence during that massage had chipped away another piece of my emotional armor.

Leaving San Francisco the next morning was difficult. Three days later I received an e-mail saying that Alisa had died, with Norman and her daughter at her side. Her daughter, sister, the attendant, and a volunteer gave her a ritual bath. Then they dressed her in a pink robe and a broad Easter hat. She would remain in the House for two days so everyone could say goodbye. I would be returning to San Francisco in three days and learn about the importance of ritual.

When I returned to the Guest House three days later, I immediately went to Alisa's room. I looked at the empty bed and thought about my time with her and her family. As I stood gazing, the attendant called to me from the hallway.

"Stan, can you clean the room? We'll be getting a new resident tomorrow."

"Sure."

The room had already been emptied of Alisa's possessions, revealing hundreds of candle drippings on the floor and furniture. It must have been a wonderful tribute, with a multitude of candles and sticks of incense. I realized as I looked around that removing the melted wax wouldn't be easy. But as I started to scrape each drop from the floor and furniture, the sense of loss I felt was diminishing. The slow process of cleaning somehow brought me closer to Alisa. I may not have been there for the end of her life, but the wax gave me a connection to her death. In some ways, I was participating in a ritual of my own making. As I scraped off each drop, I envisioned Alisa peacefully lying in bed wearing an elegant robe and an Easter hat, surrounded by family, friends, staff, and volunteers all celebrating her life.

I know some people dismiss rituals as just the historical trappings of ancient religions: prescribed traditional ceremonies that are often very beautiful but have little relevance to our contemporary lives. But clearly there is something universal about the performance of ceremonial acts—ritual crosses all lines, religious and nonreligious. Ritual seems to give us a fuller understanding of ourselves and of our common humanity. An act performed with a sense of ritual links us with our personal history, whether that act is done in the form of religious ceremony or is just a simple undertaking that connects us to our past.

A few months after Alisa died, I went back to the small town in eastern Pennsylvania where I had lived until I was fifteen years old. On Main Street—yes, it really was called Main Street—I found the Roxie Theater, the place I had spent most Saturday afternoons as a child. It was morning and, although the theater wasn't yet open to the public, the front door was unlocked. I walked in and asked the manager, a man who looked about my age, if he would allow me to wander through, to relive some of those joyous moments.

"Of course," he said. "I understand."

In the dimly lit theater I walked past the refreshment stand and remembered ordering a box of popcorn—extra butter, please. Then, I went through the door on the right, walked down the aisle, and found my favorite seat in the middle of the tenth row. As I settled in, I was again seven years old, and images were flooding my mind: Abbott and Costello, Hopalong Cassidy, Buck Rogers, and the *Our Gang* kids. The only things missing were the scattered Jujubes that held my Keds firmly to the floor. It was a spontaneous ritual I was performing, as sacred as any associated with a religion, one that pulled me back to an important time in my life.

From that day on, personal ritual became an integral part of my life and service in hospice. It included quiet sitting with residents, the ceremonial placement of revered objects, reciting centuries-old prayers, and the raucous retelling of stories with friends and loved ones surrounding the person who died, being always mindful of including him or her in the conversation. The rituals weren't elaborate. Sometimes I would visit an outdoor place where the resident and I had spent time together. More recently, I've been dedicating an improvised song to them on my Native American flute or *shakuhachi* (Japanese bamboo flute). Playing alone and allowing my feelings to be expressed in music connects my soul with my memories of the person who died. With music, I can span time.

Until my visit to the Roxie, I used to disregard my own

needs when I served others. I justified ignoring them because hospice volunteering wasn't supposed to be about me. But I realized that this was actually a self-protective way of minimizing the grief I felt from losing a friend. Ritual became my way of honoring the person I served, genuinely experiencing the loss, and allowing the juices that I needed for the next person I served to flow back into me. Rituals can take many forms; from the Catholic Requiem Mass to the ceremonial burning of cards containing the names of people who have died. Regardless of the form that ritual takes, I've found that some kind of ceremonial act is important in the process of grieving. Ritual brings memories of those we have loved into the present and allows us to continue on with those memories into the future.

The George Mark Children's House is a very special place. It is the first stand-alone children's hospice in the United States. The facility looks and feels like a home, with each of the nine patient rooms designed to look like a child's bedroom. Wallace was an eight-month-old with uncorrectable hydrocephaly—the inability of the brain to expel spinal fluid. By the time his mother brought him to George Mark, he was already unresponsive. Every week in a handcrafted chair we rhythmically rocked for four hours. I carefully cradled his head on my shoulder, because his neck muscles could no longer support his head's increased weight. Everyone hoped the morphine he was receiving would alleviate the pain caused by the increasing pressure on his brain. But since he was unable to communicate, we didn't know.

In the third week of his stay, his breathing became rapid and I could feel his little heart racing. Any increase in the dosage of morphine would be fatal. No amount of stroking or gently touching reduced the rapid breathing or look of discomfort. His whimpers were barely audible, and if I wasn't watching I wouldn't know they were occurring. Although the nurse told me he wasn't close to actively dying, I thought he might be, and I was anxious about being alone in the room with him, because I didn't want to be his last human contact. His mother lived sixty miles away and would be at the George Mark House that evening—but I was worried she would be too late. I'm not sure why, but I consciously slowed my breathing and shifted his body onto my chest. After twenty minutes, Wallace's breathing matched mine. He stayed in my arms for the next hour, restful and, I hoped, without pain.

How was it possible that something as ordinary as breathing could have such an impact? As someone who delighted in the complexity of language, I was amazed at the simplicity of the way mere breath could communicate and soothe. I know few people think of breath as a means of communication—before Wallace, I didn't either. Yet, breathing is so basic to life, how can it not be communicative? When he died the following week, he was in the arms of his mother.

Mike was fifteen years old with multiple birth defects and an inoperable brain tumor that was resistant to radiation and drugs.

"When you sit with him," the nurse said, "He may have severe headaches from the increasing pressure of the tumor."

I waited for her to tell me more, like something I was supposed to do to relieve it. When she was leaving the room I asked, "What should I do when it happens?" She slowly turned and with moist eyes said, "Just be with him."

Mike's body had been twisted by cerebral palsy. As he lay in the bed with his limbs rigid and bent in strange angles, I sat next to him and read from the books I was told he enjoyed. No one knew the extent of his cognitive deficits. In his file I read that he understood at a "three-year-old level." In thirty years of treating children and adults with cognitive deficits, I've never found descriptions of this type to be helpful. Just because someone tests at a three-year-old cognitive level doesn't mean they are emotionally three. How do you factor in the turmoil a fifteen-year-old has with a body that doesn't work and a mind that can't handle abstractions? I've found the pain and joy of someone with devastating neurological injuries to be just as intense as someone with a brilliant mind—maybe even more so.

I began reading "The Three Little Pigs" as if I were an actor on a stage. The pigs squealed, and the wolf huffed and puffed each line of dialogue. I was engrossed in my performance until Mike screamed. I immediately turned and saw his eyes were closed; with a clinched fist he was hitting his head in the area where the tumor was pressing. When I grabbed his hand I couldn't hold it back. Despite his atrophied muscles, his strength was surprisingly intense. I placed my other hand on the side of his head to absorb his repeated blows. After a few minutes, he became silent and his body relaxed. I hoped that would be the only episode. I started to read again, but this time without the theatrics, glancing at him every few seconds. I didn't have to wait long until the pain returned. It became cyclical for the next thirty minutes; a few minutes of agony were followed by a few minutes of relief.

By the third episode, my arm hurt and my hand was bruised. I opened his fist and wrapped his hand around mine. At first, I didn't know if he understood that I wanted him to squeeze my hand instead of hitting himself. But seconds before the next episode, I could feel his fingers tightening, then just like before, the shrieking pain came, but now instead of banging his head, he squeezed my hand harder than I could have imagined possible from any fifteen-year-old with cerebral palsy.

All through my life, I had relied on language to console someone's pain or loss. But with Mike, language would have been futile. From him, I learned that for some of the most basic needs, there is no substitute for a simple action. And looking back, I had a new perspective on times when I might have shown compassion just by holding a person, instead of searching for words that were never adequate.

When I was nine years old, my parents owned a grocery store in our small town in Pennsylvania, which was populated by Eastern European immigrants. We lived upstairs, and my mother would often call me down to play my accordion for customers. The most frequent requests were "The Beer Barrel Polka," "The Marines' Hymn," and "She's Too Fat for Me." If I felt especially courageous I would spontaneously let loose with "Lady of Spain," which always required you to shake the bellows (the flexible folds between the two halves of the accordion), making you appear as if you were having a seizure. I hated playing publicly then, and even years later I was never really good enough to play for people with any instrument I tried. But things were different one day at George Mark, when a five-year-old child named Alice, who was expected to die within the month, was restless and couldn't be comforted.

Because of a severe brain injury that cut off oxygen to her brain, she was profoundly deaf, totally blind, and cognitively unresponsive. According to her mother, Alice connected with the world only through touch and smell. Nothing we did that day seemed to help. Not the fragrant flowers held under her nose, the scented water gently sprayed on her face, or cradling, which in the past had always worked. I watched her writhing movements and felt helpless. Although I dreaded playing publicly, I thought music might help. Reluctantly, I went to my car and brought back a Native American flute.

It's a simple six-holed instrument made of wood that can be traced back to the Anasazi Indians in the United States around 1200 B.C.E. A similar forty-thousand-year-old instrument made from a bear's leg bone was found in a Mongolian cave. Native Americans called them "love flutes" and only played them as part of a courting ritual. The songs, played only by men, were intended to convey emotions that were forbidden for public display. Going back into Alice's room, I closed the door so nobody would hear. I had been playing for less than three months, and my wife cringed whenever she heard me practice. I thought a closed door would prevent the embarrassment I would feel if the staff heard my screeching mistakes. I had momentarily forgotten that once on a hike in

Rocky Mountain National Park, I had been heard playing this flute a quarter mile away. Wendy, who was hiking some distance in front of me, described how a family came to a complete stop and listened, not moving as long as they could hear the music. When I stopped playing, they moved on. But as soon as I resumed, they would again stop and listen. Wendy said it was as if they "just had to stop and listen appreciatively," even though, she added, "You really don't play that well!"

I began to play softly for Alice. None of the songs I had memorized came out. Instead, notes seemed to magically string themselves together, creating a tune I had never played or even heard before. *Where did this music come from?*

Playing with my eyes closed, I was no longer conscious of what I was doing. For the first time in my life I felt a connection with the music I was playing. When I opened my eyes, I saw Alice's head following the flute as I played. She started to relax and eventually fell asleep. There was something primal in Alice's reaction. I knew it wasn't my musical ability. As I left her room, I saw that the staff had gathered in the hallway. Through the open doorway they saw that Alice was finally sleeping.

"Could you play again next week for the other children?" asked a nurse. I did bring my flute and played the following week, and after that music became a regular part of my hospice service, not only with children but also adults.

In *This Is Your Brain on Music,* Daniel Levitin presented a compelling argument that neurologically our brains are wired to connect more with music than with words. I think there is a primacy in music that expresses feelings that may be too threatening or embarrassing to communicate in words. At least for me that is true. I've found that there are times when I'm playing the flute when I can tap into feelings that don't have words or that I may be reluctant to talk about. But through music, they're there; accessible, immediate, and always poignant.

Communication from the heart provided me with a newfound gift—an unflagging honesty that wasn't hindered by concerns about my image or the consequences of my actions. Maybe this kind of honesty is what we are all capable of, before our maturing mind starts exerting control over how we present ourselves to the world. When I was seven, I wasn't afraid of sitting in a darkened theater having unfiltered experiences; I never wondered if what I was feeling or saying was appropriate. At seven, I rejoiced in who I was. But with age and sophistication come a more complicated way of viewing life, guided by social rules of behavior and the ability to nuance the honesty out of words.

In many ways, the nature of how emotional honesty diminishes over time is a lot like the growth of cataracts: starting slowly, they grow for years unnoticed because the change is so subtle, until one day, you realize your vision has become clouded. It's an overnight realization of a state that may have taken years to arrive at. What I viewed as a protective device—emotional armor—was my own cataract, clouding my view of reality and separating me from people who were offering help.

5

Faces of Compassion

When we harm others we are harming
ourselves;
and when we take care of others,
we are taking care of ourselves.

—Akong Tulku Rinpoche

There is no one way to display "compassion." At the Zen Hospice Project's Guest House I learned to express it in *how* I did things, not in what I did. I could be cooking dinner at five o'clock, feeding a resident at six o'clock, helping an attendant change a diaper at seven o'clock, spending time at eight o'clock talking about life and death with a resident, and taking care of a backed-up toilet at nine o'clock. All very different activities, yet each was done to provide comfort. The way we cared for the residents was based on a model of compassion that had been integral to the hospice since its founding, more than twenty years ago. Aside from being a physical home for those who were dying, it also was the core social setting for many who cared for them. The place was an ocean of compassion, with its waters healing both those who were cared for and those doing the caring. Spirituality was renewed, meaning was put back into lives, relationships were developed, problems solved, and heartbreaks consoled. So, when we learned the hospice might close, everyone was devastated.

The House's insurance company presented a list of eighty-four repair items to the director that needed to be completed in thirty days or the insurance would be cancelled.

"We're sorry," the insurance agent said, "but since nine-eleven, we can't be too careful."

That was the only explanation offered. There were no prior warnings and, what was most inexplicable, there had never been an insurance claim since the House opened. Other insurance companies were contacted, but all declined to insure the House. The director pleaded for a three-month extension—enough time for the two remaining residents to die. The answer was an unequivocal "no." It would take at least two years to do the necessary repairs—at a cost of $600,000, which the House didn't have. And obtaining a license for a new facility would take even longer. The residents, who were close to death, would have to be moved. When the director was notified of the carrier's decision, no new residents were admitted. The House had been full a few weeks back. But with four recent deaths, only two residents remained.

I tried to imagine what the residents were feeling by putting myself in their place—something I've always found helped me develop compassion. Let's say I had, at the most, six months to live—a requirement of entering all hospice programs—and my family had been searching for a facility since the prognosis. I've been placed on several waiting lists, but there are five people waiting for each available bed, so meanwhile I might die at home or in a hospital. My family can't care for me at home, and I dread dying amid the sterility and clamor of a hospital. Then, as if my prayers have been answered, a bed is offered to me at the Zen Project's Guest House, one of the most honored hospices in the country. Although I'm relieved, I know that the cost of my good fortune was someone's death. As I'm wheeled over the threshold into the House, it finally hits me that there is no hope for my recovery.

The Guest House will be my final home. It's not my real home, and no matter how compassionate the caregivers might be and how beautiful my room is, my initial reaction is, "This isn't where I want to die." Not in a strange house, populated by people I don't have a history with. Not in a bed I know countless people have lain in as they died.

I want my own bed, in my own room. My contradictory feelings of wanting to be here and not wanting to be are legitimized when I'm told it's the rare person who initially welcomes the move, even those who lived in squalor. I finally settle in, as if I'm sinking into a comfortable chair with the stuffing moving to fit each part of my body. I say to myself, "It will be all right to die here, right here in this bed." But now I have to move. That's the scenario I thought the residents would be facing. The hospice board decided that although the residents' families, along with hospice volunteers and staff, would be kept informed as each alternative was eliminated, Nick and Mary wouldn't be told until there truly were no options.

"Not a bad place if you're going to die," Nick often said when he was the recipient of any gesture of kindness. A left-handed compliment was the best he could give. Nick was fifty-three and had lived with hepatitis C for ten years. He was fond of wearing anything outrageous, and recently he'd had his hair bleached white one day, followed by a carrot-orange the next. When he came to the House, he was demanding of everyone. Nothing was right. Not the food preparation, not the way his laundry was folded, not even the efforts of volunteers, some of whom he drove to tears. But gradually over the next two months, he changed. He not only wanted to do everything by himself, but he also offered to help volunteers and staff. I would often come in early and see Nick doing other residents' laundry. He would console relatives and sit by the bedside comforting people who were closer to death than he. At other times, he would assist in cleaning and dressing residents. Nick had been a registered nurse in the AIDS unit of San Francisco General during its worst epidemic years, and he knew more about the medical aspects of his illness than those who cared for him.

As his heart became more open, his body deteriorated. A national organization was planning to award him for his lifelong contributions to the gay, lesbian, and transgender community at an awards banquet. A few weeks before the banquet I overheard a conversation Nick had with some of his many friends who would visit him. "You'd better stay alive until the banquet," one friend said. Everyone laughed except Nick.

With a smile he said, "I'll do my best."

A few days before the award he asked me to take him shopping for a new shirt. He wanted to "knock their eyes out."

He pulled four large neon-colored shirts from the rack and went into a fitting room. As I waited outside, I heard him faintly calling.

"Stan," he said from behind the closed door, "could you give me a hand?"

I opened the door and saw he was sitting down and attempting to unbutton his shirt. While his fingers could grasp the button, he couldn't withdraw it from the buttonhole. While I gently unbuttoned and removed his shirt, he kept looking at the floor. After I put on a bright-yellow neon shirt and buttoned it, he slowly stood and peered into the mirror. He looked like a young child trying on his father's clothing. For what seemed like an eternity, he stared at himself in the mirror.

"Could you get me the same colors, but in medium?" he eventually asked as his eyes teared up.

"Sure Nick."

I returned the large shirts and brought him the mediums. After helping him close the buttons he again looked in the mirror. These shirts were also too large. He scanned his body as I lifted his arms to remove the shirt. Without saying anything, I took the mediums back and returned with smalls.

"Let's try these," I said.

The first one I helped him into fit perfectly.

"Do you want to try on the others?" I asked.

"No. Oh Christ."

We silently drove back to the House with three outrageously colored shirts.

• • •

Mary was seventy-four and always wore elegant nightgowns, the type you often see in 1930s movies. The silk flowed over her body, rendering the large tumor on her abdomen less obvious. When I first met her a few days after she arrived, she was critical of almost everything I did. I couldn't make her breakfast in the "right way" or bring up the newspaper quickly enough. But everything changed after I cleaned the chandelier because of an offhand comment she made about its globes being dusty. It was a simple gesture, one I didn't give much thought to, but it seemed to be the turning point in our relationship. In the weeks that followed I learned of disturbing events in her past. She would let something leak out with the same emotion one read an account of the weather. "Oh, yes," she said when I described the pain I experienced from the fractured pelvis. "I bet that hurt more than my broken leg." When I asked how that happened, she casually said, "Oh, my father threw me out of the window when I was five. How about making me one of your special milkshakes?"

In spite of Nick's outrageous behavior and his anti-straight comments, and Mary's conservative views, they became close—the middle-class matron and the flamboyant gay founder of a historical art collection. To those of us who cared for them, it appeared that their lives were tied together by a common denominator: both came to the House bitter, both were becoming softer as they approached death. What we didn't realize at the time was what was causing it. The changes weren't linear; often sweetness and sarcasm would be mixed together, sometimes even within the same sentence. One afternoon when I was sitting with Mary, Nick peeked into the room and watched us until Mary saw him.

"Well, what do you want?" she said to him in a way that sounded annoyed unless you knew her.

"Here," he said, as he entered the room. "I know you like them." He threw a box of chocolates on the bed and left. By the time Mary picked up the box and put on her glasses, he was walking down the hallway.

"I'm glad you got me See's," she yelled. "If they were something else, you'd have to eat them all. Every last one of them!"

I couldn't hear Nick's complete response, but I thought I heard the word "witch." Neither Nick nor Mary was good at expressing emotions. Nick eventually told me that no matter how hard he tried, he couldn't leave behind a lifetime of unfulfilled relationships, and as a result, any comments that made him vulnerable could rarely be said without sarcasm. He felt he always had to hold back a little, "just in case."

For the first time, many of us wished our two friends a speedy death. But it didn't happen. I was sitting with Mary when she noticed the strings on my wrist.

"They're called protection strings," I said.

"Why?"

"They've been blessed by a person of great spiritual awareness. I don't know who blessed these, but I was told it was a high lama."

"How did you get them?"

"When I wasn't doing well physically, friends who were Buddhists sent them to me."

"And what about now?"

"I'm doing better."

She leaned back in her chair and nodded her head.

"I have another one at home," I said. "Would you like it?"

"Yes, very much so," she said softly.

I came back the next day with my last unused protection string. "This should stay on until it disintegrates," I said as I tied it to her wrist.

"Or until they burn me up," she quipped. "You know, I noticed we haven't gotten anyone new for a few weeks. With such a shortage of hospice beds, why do you think nobody has come in?" I dreaded this question, since I knew I couldn't tell her the truth and I've always been an unconvincing liar.

"I don't know," I said, relieved when she didn't pursue my answer.

I kissed her goodbye and left. It was Tuesday and I would return on Thursday when they would be told. Mary's daughter and Nick's sister had to decide if they or the director would tell them. Nick's sister had arrived earlier in the week for the awards ceremony and was staying with him in his room. She decided to have the director do it while she was present. The decision for Mary's daughter was more complex. It was only on Jill's insistence that Mary had come to the Guest House in the first place. Jill was afraid that her mother—who had always been critical in the past—would accuse her of having made the wrong decision. Jill decided to have the director tell Mary alone, then she would come into the room and talk to her mother.

On Thursday morning tissue boxes were being used by everyone in the House. The night before, Nick had received his award. Volunteers sat in the kitchen with Mary's daughter and some of the staff. Just as in most homes, the kitchen was a comfortable place where the most important discussions were usually held. It was always warmer than the rest of the house, and because the stove's exhaust hood didn't work, cooking odors lingered for days. That morning we agreed to follow Nick and Mary, if not as hospice volunteers then as friends who would be with them until they died. We had finished serving them breakfast, and as I washed the dishes I felt as if I had entered some sort of a trance state. I knew people were talking, but I couldn't understand the words. All I could hear was the hum of the refrigerator and the spurts of the coffee machine. I wondered what I could find to replace the most fulfilling thing I had ever done; something that was changing my life. My concerns for Nick and Mary returned when I heard the nurse coming down the stairs.

"He's with Mary now," she said. "Then he'll tell Nick."

She poured herself a cup of coffee and silently joined us. I tried to imagine what words he would use to minimize the distress of the decision. Would he try to say that there were other places that would be just as nice? Would he take a more honest approach and simply confront the loss? Or would he take an approach that was more spiritual, trying to turn lemons into lemonade? We sat around the table as if we were mourning the death of a loved one, when I heard movement from upstairs.

"Stan. Can you come up here?" the attendant called from the top of the stairs. "Mary wants to walk."

It was Mary's way of dealing with anxiety. Usually the halting movements of her emaciated legs, unsteadily placing one foot three inches in front of another, provided some peace. When I arrived in front of her room, the door was open and she was sitting in a chair crying.

"It's not fair. It's not fair," she kept repeating as I went to her side and hugged her. Recently, she had decided there was no longer any need for modesty. She wore only a Hawaiian shirt and a diaper.

"Mary, no matter where you'll go, we'll be there. We'll be with you until the end."

"But it's so beautiful here. This is where I want to die, nowhere else."

Although there were non-hospice facilities in the Bay Area that could have cared for her, none of the dedicated hospice sites had any beds available, and all had long waiting lists. Everyone realized that neither Nick nor Mary would probably have enough time to move up the lists. The only facilities with immediate openings were skilled nursing homes. Although some were considered "first-rate," their reputation was based on their newness, or quality of food, or cost, or physical environment, or patient-staff ratio. There was no rating for compassion; the only thing both Nick and Mary wanted.

"I have to walk now," Mary said.

I helped her out of the chair and held her arm as we moved out into the hall. She carefully placed one foot down after the other, all the time with tears flowing down her checks. Our walk only lasted until the end of the hallway. When we returned to her room, her daughter entered. They embraced, and Jill tried to console her.

"Would you like some tea?" I asked Mary.

She nodded yes. When I left their room, I could see that Nick's door was still closed.

"How are they doing?" the volunteers in the kitchen asked when I came back down.

"He's telling Nick now. Mary's devastated. I think after she's had time with Jill, she probably would like to see everyone."

I returned with the tea and placed it next to Mary. Jill was trying to comfort her mother by caressing her and repeatedly saying, "It will be all right, Mother. You'll see, it will be fine."

"No, it won't. It can't be," Mary said between sobs.

There were no recriminations as Jill feared. I didn't know if that was because she had misread her mother or because this was such a traumatic event that pointing fingers would be superfluous.

"Would you like some time alone with Jill?" I asked.

"Yes," Mary responded.

When I left, I decided to wait outside Nick's room until his door opened. When the director left I said, "May I come in?" Nick nodded "yes" without looking up. Through the open door I saw he was sitting on the edge of a bench, his head bowed and his eyes closed. His sister was sitting next to him on a couch. He had filled his large room with almost everything of importance from his apartment. There were pictures mounted on the wall, boxes of archival notes, small unrelated objects, and in the corner was a figure he called "Timmy," a three-foot-high three-dimensional plastic boy.

"I'm sorry Nick."

"Yeah, but what are you going to do?"

He had been stoic throughout his stay, often making comments about his health and eventual death with as much seriousness as a host on a late-night comedy show discusses politics. Everyone was worried he would be upset about having to move to a facility where the enormous number of possessions he'd brought with him wouldn't be allowed. He had told me that having his things with him not only gave him comfort but helped him hold on to life. "You're not going to get rid of us, Nick. Just my cooking." He laughed. I had been the butt of his jokes since he arrived; he called my cooking simple, plain, barely acceptable, and—when he was feeling particularly mean—"on par with the best of McDonalds."

"I think I'd like to go outside and sit in the sun," Nick said.

When we were in front of Mary's room, I asked him if he wanted to visit with her. Volunteers had come to her room and were unsuccessfully trying to console her.

"What!" he said loudly, "you want me to talk to that old witch?" Mary stopped crying and laughed. He stepped a few feet into her room and, after looking at her for a few moments, he said, "Wherever I'm going, you'd better come with me." Then he paused before softly saying, "I need you."

"And I need you too," Mary retorted, without the slightest hint of sarcasm.

There were six people in the room, and all of us were crying. It was something we rarely did in front of residents. It wasn't that we were devoid of emotion. Rather, the presence of a volunteer is often a major calming influence for residents and their families. Our role was to support, not participate. But on many occasions, such as this one, the line between the two dissolved. Nick asked me to help him downstairs into the garden. With one hand he held on to the banister and placed his other hand on my shoulder. I wouldn't describe his grasp as affectionate, but neither was it just for physical support. The garden, as most found in the back of Victorian homes in San Francisco, was pocket-sized, with every available space planted with shade-tolerant flowers and bushes. When we arrived, I saw that two volunteers, Mary's daughter, and Nick's sister were already gathered in the only area where the sun was still shining. Nick and I sat down, not saying anything. I smelled a mixture of sweet fragrances coming from the garden and felt guilty about taking pleasure in it. No one talked, but everyone except Nick kept glancing at each other with a look that I interpreted as a plea to "make it right."

After about ten minutes one of the volunteers looked down the path to the house and said, "Well, look who's coming!" It was Mary, supported by the nurse. Her eyes were hidden by large sunglasses and the only clothes she wore were the Hawaiian shirt and the diaper. Her pink slippers, which could have been worn to a formal event, enabled her to shuffle along. When she finally reached us, I placed a cushion on the wooden chair next to Nick. She sat down and crossed her legs.

"Wasilla," she said, looking like a scantily clothed Greta Garbo. We looked at her, not understanding the reference until she gestured to the fifty-year-old bush climbing up the back of the house. We all silently looked at it as Nick and Mary, without touching, leaned their bodies closer to each other. As the sun went behind the adjoining building, the garden, which moments before was pleasant, became intolerably cold for them. Nick left unaccompanied, insisting that he could walk by himself. Mary, however, needed help from both the nurse and me. Even with us supporting her, we only made it to the porch landing. Mary was completely exhausted as the nurse and I gently lowered her onto a chair. Jill came over and knelt in front of her, clasping both of Mary's hands in hers.

"It's not fair," Mary again said.

"No, Mom, it's worse than that. It's fucked!"

"Well, Mary," I said, "can't you do a little better than 'not fair'?"

"It's damn shitty," she said, almost smiling.

Two days later I left for a ten-day lecture tour in Taiwan; I wouldn't be back before the House closed. With my presentation schedule, I had only a limited amount of free time to find an Internet connection. And when I did have time, I couldn't access an English-language site. With the difference in time, telephoning was impossible. The images of that last day stayed with me, often surfacing in the middle of a lecture. I would look out into the audience and see someone who reminded me of Nick or Mary. Even a swatch of orange on someone's shirt brought back memories.

When I returned to San Francisco, I learned Mary and Nick decided that they would only move to a facility that could house both of them. When nothing could be found,

Nick offered to pay for an apartment for the two of them—something that wasn't medically possible, since both were fragile and their medications needed to be constantly monitored. Eventually a room was found in the basement of a nursing home three blocks from the hospice. The small room was actually an alcove off a large meeting room. The eight-by-fifteen-foot area was transformed into a bedroom as a courtesy to the Zen Hospice Project. It not only stood in contrast spatially with the meeting room, but also in lighting. Whereas the alcove was brightly lit, the meeting room was perpetually dim. The administrators of the facility knew the story of the hospice's insurance problems and offered to do whatever was necessary to keep Mary and Nick together. While the nursing home provided the physical space, it was the hospice staff and volunteers who would care for them. With one narrow bed near each side wall, the aisle between them was less than three feet wide. Everything on Mary's side was neat and arranged by categories. Shirts on the top, pants to the right, personal hygiene to the left. It stood in contrast with Nick's part of the room. He was allowed to bring only a few possessions with him. Interspersed with jumbled piles of clothing and toiletries were computer parts and stacked boxes.

Mary was no longer walking when I returned, and she was now wearing plain bathrobes. On her better days, when I could convince her to wear pants and a coat, I took her and Nick out of the facility to one of the neighborhood's coffee shops. All of Nick's clothes, even the small neon-colored shirts, were now too large for him and he no longer had his friend touch up his hair color. I noticed his belt had a new hole punched in it, and even on this last hole the belt barely held up his pants. He was still ambulatory, and when Mary was too weak to go outside or preferred to sleep, Nick and I took rides to various places around San Francisco where he could smoke his medical marijuana and talk about his life. Even though I was scheduled to come in only on Tuesday mornings, I also visited when I knew no other volunteers could be there. On one visit, Mary started having problems with her breathing. Even with additional medication, it remained labored and shallow.

"The cancer has metastasized to her lungs," the nurse explained. "I think it's getting close."

On the next day when I visited, Nick had been in pain for most of the day, and he was finally sleeping with the help of medication. Mary was lying in her bed breathing heavily. Her eyes were closed, and she didn't acknowledge me.

"She's starting to go," the attendant said. "At the most, a few days."

As I looked at her, I remembered the milkshakes I made for her, her love of crossword puzzles, our silently drinking coffee in the morning, and then everything that occurred when she learned the House was closing. The attendant and I sat by Mary's side and talked about how important knowing her had been to us; we constantly included her in our conversation even though we had no idea if she could hear us. I had errands to do that couldn't wait, so I thought I would stop in early the next morning to say my final goodbye. The attendant felt confident that Mary would still be alive then. I completed all of my tasks by 5:00 P.M. and I was on my way home when I felt a sudden urge to return to the facility. I can't explain it, but

I had similar feelings before when someone in hospice died. I turned my car around and began speeding through the streets of San Francisco.

When I arrived, Sam, one of the volunteers, was at Mary's bedside. Her breathing was heavier, with a rattling noise on each exhalation. More ominous were the short pauses between breaths.

The attendant, who was sitting in the adjoining room, said that Mary's daughter Jill had just left for a quick dinner and would return shortly. When he came into the room and saw Mary's breathing, he immediately called Jill. She didn't answer her cell phone, so he left a message that her mother had taken a turn for the worse and she should return as soon as possible. Sam and I remained at Mary's side and each held a hand. Jean, another volunteer who had felt an urge similar to mine, arrived and joined us. Together, we stood vigil. There were now longer pauses between breaths, and the flow of breath had calmed. I turned around and saw Nick was still asleep.

"Nick," I said gently touching his shoulder, "I think she's beginning to go."

"Thanks," he said. He stood up unsteadily, then walked to the foot of her bed. Nick's poker face never changed; not even then, when we all knew it was only minutes before Mary would die. We hoped her daughter would make it in time. Although I knew Nick hadn't been present when anyone at the House died, I thought he must have witnessed it often as a nurse. I wondered if he thought he was watching a reflection of his own death. The effortful breathing diminished, as did the rattling, and Mary's face lost all its tension. With her final exhalation everything in the room seemed to change. I couldn't hear anything. The air seemed to stop moving, and colors appeared more brilliant. Whether what I experienced had a physical reality or whether my mind just imagined it happening, I'll never know. I no longer wondered if Nick was seeing his death in Mary—I began envisioning my own. Nick stood back and watched as each of us in turn said our final goodbye and kissed her on the forehead. When we finished, Nick slowly sat down on his bed and looked at Mary without saying anything or touching her.

The attendant called the nurse, who arrived shortly. She told us Mary had requested that a ritual bath be performed for her, similar to the one done for another resident. It was one used for centuries by Native Americans in preparing their dead. The first step, with the nurse's guidance, was cleaning her body. We would only clean it and then wait to see if Jill wished to participate in the rest of the ritual. As we gently washed Mary's body, I felt as if I was cleaning the body of one of my children when they were infants. With my children and Mary, there was only love that flowed from my hands. Smells from bodily functions that I would have been repulsed by in other situations were just part of life, and now death. Once Mary's body was cleaned, Jean and Sam said they had to leave for another hospice assignment.

"I'll stay with Mary until Jill arrives," I said.

We were very protective of bodies. After a person died, there was always someone present until family arrived or it was removed to a mortuary. In some ways, the dead, who were totally defenseless, required more compassion than that given to the living. Nick had left the alcove unnoticed and was in the shadows of the adjoining room. He walked from one side of the room to the other, his eyes fixed on the floor. Jill arrived and saw the expressions of the volunteers and staff who had gathered when they learned about Mary. She ran into the alcove where she saw her mother covered with a quilt up to her chest, her hands folded, and almost smiling. It was only then that she realized her mother had died. Her cell phone had been turned off and she never received the attendant's message.

"I should have been here," she repeatedly said through sobs. "I didn't have to go out to eat. I should have been here."

"Quite often," the nurse said, "people who are dying will wait until their loved ones aren't present. Some believe this is their way of sparing them the pain of witnessing their death. Sometimes, in spite of maintaining a vigil near the end of someone's life, the person lets go when the loved one takes a break for only a short time."

Jill stopped crying and looked back at her mother. "Yes, that's something I'd expect her to do now, but never before." It wouldn't be until later that evening I learned what she meant.

"Would you like to participate in the ceremonial bath?" the nurse asked.

"I don't know. Do you think I should?" she asked me. Jill and I had spent much time together since her mother arrived at the House, and in the past, just as now, she felt more comfortable asking me for advice than I felt giving it.

"I don't think there's any right or wrong," the nurse said when she saw I was struggling to form an answer. "But it's helped other people to deal with the grief they felt. Why don't you start and if it's too painful, you can just stop and we'll continue."

"I think I'd like that," Jill said.

The combination of herbs and plants were assembled according to an ancient formula. They were placed into a bowl of hot water and, just like a fine tea, allowed to steep. The rising steam carried a subtle odor throughout the alcove as the nurse handed Jill a white cloth that had been dipped into the solution. As she lovingly cleaned her mother's face, she began talking to her.

"I hope you're finally at peace, Mom. I know how hard it's been for you. I know I've done things that have disappointed you, but I always loved you. I'm sorry for hurting you. I never meant to."

Three of us took our cloths and washed other parts of Mary's body over the next fifteen minutes, as Jill softly asked her mother for forgiveness. After she finished cleaning her mother's face, she kissed her on the lips and turned to us for the first time since the ritual bath began. It was only then that she saw our tears.

"Thank you for doing this for her and for me," she said.

Earlier, the nurse had laid out Mary's favorite set of pajamas. It was a light yellow pastel color with pictures of surfers and 1950s cars.

"What do you think, Mom? Would you like these?" Jill asked.

We all laughed and agreed that these were her favorites. Nick, unnoticed, had quietly returned to the room.

"The only problem I see," he said, standing in the corner in front of Timmy, "is you're putting on the bottoms. You know how much she loved showing off her legs."

As everyone laughed, the attendant asked Jill to join him in the adjacent room. I accompanied her.

"The mortuary wants to know when they should come for Mary," he said. "Do you want her to stay until morning so that more people can visit?" It was the usual procedure that when someone died an e-mail was sent to all staff and volunteers inviting them to say goodbye. Jill thought about it as she glanced back into the bedroom.

"No, I think we should have them come for her this evening. I don't want Nick to be here with her all night."

An e-mail was immediately sent to staff and volunteers inviting them to an impromptu memorial at Mary's bedside. We would have almost two hours to be with her and say goodbye. We dressed her in her favorite Hawaiian pajamas—including the pants—and placed a rose in her hands. Petals from the flowers in the room were placed between her toes, and following an Indian tradition, sage was gently nestled into her ears to create a sacred smoke during her cremation. I hoped my protection string would also help her on her journey. For the next hour volunteers and staff who cared for Mary at the Guest House streamed in to say goodbye. Three of us sat on Nick's bed, others stood, and Jill sat on the floor affectionately stroking her mother's leg. Nick had stayed in the corner, but now he was standing next to Timmy with his hand on his head. Everyone except Jill and Nick shared memories of Mary. Mine was the chandelier story. Many of the recollections were similar—a story of someone who was bitter, then within a short period of time became as loving as the grandmother we all wished we'd had. Eventually, Jill, who had been silent during our stories, spoke.

"You may not have known it, but Mom had a rough life."

For more than thirty minutes Jill told us about her mother's experiences, which began on the plains of Nebraska. At age fifteen Mary had run away from a dysfunctional family, then went through three crushing love affairs, after which she became a reclusive alcoholic. For ten years, she never left her house, drinking herself into oblivion, often not even allowing her daughter to enter. Jill emphasized that prior to coming to the Guest House, she couldn't remember more than a few instances when Mary was happy. It was as if her past stood behind her creating a shadow that dominated everything. This person described by Jill bore no resemblance to the woman we had cared for and had grown to love.

"She didn't want to come to the House," Jill said. "We fought bitterly over it. Even though she didn't like the care facility she was in, at least she was familiar with it. Though I hadn't visited the Guest House, I heard about what went on there. I told her that's where she was going and there would be no further discussion. But there was more discussion. She brought up everything wrong I ever did and kept accusing me of deliberately hurting her. I knew it was her past talking, but I couldn't do anything about it. I felt as if the drunken recluse was right there again."

"But that wasn't the woman we knew," one of the volunteers said.

"No, the woman you knew was the person you created." I didn't know what Jill meant by this. It couldn't be that she thought we were delusional, imagining qualities that weren't there.

"You transformed her with your kindness," Jill said. "Two weeks before the House closed we were talking about what all of you meant to her and how you made her approaching death easier to accept. With two months of compassion you made her forget a lifetime of misery. At the end of our conversation she said to me, 'Where were these people all my life?'"

Shortly after Mary died, a bed opened up for Nick at Coming Home Hospice, and I spent every Friday there with him. I usually arrived by ten and we would spend the day roaming around San Francisco.

"Hey, Nick, any place special today?"

"Nope. You have something in mind?"

"Yeah, a place called Bean Hollow."

He looked at me as if I'd said something ridiculous.

"Where, or what, is it?"

"You'll see," I said, heading in the direction of the ocean.

The fog burned off as we drove south on the Pacific Coast Highway. To our left were towering cliffs and on the right, battered rocks jetting out of the water. Nick was quiet. I thought it could have been the pain or just another bad night. As I was about to say something, I remembered something I had read in the classic book by the Tibetan Buddhist teacher Sogyal Rinpoche, *The Tibetan Book of Living and Dying*. He said, "Lecturing is for entertainment, silence for deep learning." I continued driving and waited for Nick to say something. His weight was still dropping, and his cheeks were hollow. After fifteen minutes he spoke.

"I'm afraid now."

"Afraid of dying?"

"No. Afraid I'll continue to live."

"I don't understand."

"Look, I should have been dead months ago. Yet, here I am." He turned toward to his right, to the ocean. I saw he was crying. "You folks have been incredible to me. So have my friends and family. But everyone thought I only had weeks to live. How much more can I expect everyone to put out? What I'm afraid of is that I'll outlive the kindness."

He looked forward, waiting for me to respond.

"Remember what you said last week? That we were different from paid staff because we didn't have to be kind to you? That we did it because we wanted to?"

"Yes, but there's limits, you know."

"Not for us, but maybe for you."

"Now I don't understand."

"Do you think you're the only one who gets something out of us being compassionate to you?" He still looked confused. "Do you really think we do this because we're such great people? That we swim in altruism? I don't. Sometimes, you're a royal pain in the ass."

He smiled, and then laughed.

"Why would I take your abuse and come back for more if I wasn't getting something out of it?"

"Because you're a masochist?"

"I do it because a day doesn't go by when after I leave you I don't learn something about myself. I'm with you every week, not because I like you, but because I'm a selfish son of a bitch." We both laughed hysterically.

"But I do like you," I said.

"So, tell me about this Bean Hollow place we're going to."

"When a friend of mine's son died, we took his ashes there and dropped them into the ocean."

"In case you haven't noticed, I'm still alive."

"We're going there because I think it's one of the most beautiful places I've ever been, and I'm tired of sitting on a bench at Land's End watching you smoke pot."

"You know you're always welcome."

"That's all I need. To be busted with someone who says he has a prescription for his grass." He smiled, realizing I never did believe him.

We pulled into the parking lot, and I came around to Nick's door so I could undo his seatbelt. He looked at a rock mound fifty feet from the shoreline and watched waves breaking over the sixty-foot-high edge. To the right was a bed of seaweed gently rolling with each wave. To the left were a series of tide pools, and beyond them seal lions were nursing their pups on shallow rock ledges.

"I'd like to go down to the tide pools," he said, as I watched him descend a steep trail.

"Nick! Let me help you down."

It was too late. He slid down the sand path and looked up at me as if I was a parent who couldn't prevent their child from doing something dangerous. We walked along the pools, Nick plunging his hands into the water then holding them to his nose and licking the water off his fingers. We walked back up the path, and when it got steep I placed my hands on Nick's behind and pushed. At the top of the path was a picnic table.

"Want to sit?" I asked.

Barely able to breathe, he said, "You bet."

"I understand you're going back to your sister's house in Detroit for a couple of weeks."

"I leave Wednesday. I don't know about the two weeks though. I can see why you chose this place. Maybe I should have some of my ashes thrown into that tide pool? Sure smelled good."

We drove back without talking. When I said goodbye to him inside the hospice, he hugged me. It was only the second time I could remember him doing that. But this time he kissed me on the cheek and said, "Thanks, Stan," before walking back to his room without letting me say anything. That was the last time I saw Nick. He died peacefully one week later with his sister at his side.

Before coming to hospice, I had falsely assumed that being compassionate was effortful and related to "big" things. But it's not. There is a story of an old man who tries to save a scorpion on a branch that overhangs a swiftly flowing river. Each time he tries to rescue the scorpion, it stings him. A man on shore is watching and eventually says to the old man, "You stupid old man, don't you know you could kill yourself by trying to save that ungrateful scorpion?" The man replies,

"Just because it is the scorpion's nature to sting, that does not change my nature to save."

It seemed to me that when I let go of my ego-based agenda, a new or maybe just a fresh person emerged, for whom the ability to be compassionate took no greater effort than to breathe. I was just being human. I became kind, not because I had an ulterior motive but because I couldn't do anything else. And it wasn't just me. Everyone, from nurses to the person who cleaned the floors, displayed it. After Mary and Nick died, I became more aware of the changes that occurred in new patients I served. What they were experiencing was rare—a total immersion in a sea of compassion. It was transforming not only for them, but for everyone who witnessed or participated in it.

6

The Dilemma of Hope

> If you lose hope, somehow you lose the vitality that keeps life moving, you lose that courage to be, that quality that helps you go on in spite of it all. And so today I still have a dream.
>
> —Martin Luther King Jr.

> Hope . . . is the worst of all evils, for it prolongs the torments of man.
>
> —Friedrich Nietzsche

I think the word "hope," or at least the concept of it, must have been first developed by prehistoric people cowering in their caves at night, wondering if the sun would rise the next day. With no control over a phenomenon that was so central to their lives, there was nothing else to do but hope. Without hope, there would be no letup from the fear of being devoured by unseen animals. When the sun did rise the next morning, they must have been relieved but still unsure how it happened. *Did we do that by intensely wishing it to happen?* They hoped for a repetition the next night, and the next and the next. Watch a person playing a slot machine in Las Vegas as they tap a coin three times on their lucky bracelet before dropping it into the machine, and you'll witness a modern version of the caveman's hope.

The sun rising for prehistoric people, three cherries in a row for an inveterate gambler, and living cancer-free for me; we all hope for a good outcome over something we believe we have no control over. Hope allowed me to feel I might live longer than the statistics suggested. But the more I hoped, the less I did; there was no reason to rush, there would always be tomorrow, and the next day, and well, you get the picture. I faced a dilemma. On one hand I could blithely go through life hoping the dice were rolling in my favor. If I was wrong, I probably would not have enough time to tie up the loose ends necessary for a "good" death. On the other hand, if I abandoned hope and prepared to die even though there were no current indications that my death was remotely imminent, would I be needlessly fabricating a depressing life that might go on for a long time? I searched from something in between—a middle ground. I found it with Joyce's help.

Joyce was sixty-two and had been a successful manager for a small company. I learned her history during a phone call with her sister to schedule a visit. One morning she was surprised when she had difficulty buttoning her blouse with her left hand. Thinking nothing of it, she switched to her right hand and attributed the problem to "too many tequila shots" the night before. When the same problem occurred while she was putting in her contact lenses, her concern increased. She realized something was seriously wrong when she slurred her words during her first conversation at work. The diagnosis was glioblastoma, an aggressive form of brain cancer. Surgery was scheduled within two weeks, and most of the tumor was removed. The surgeon told Joyce's sister that she had a maximum of eighteen months to live.

The surgery left Joyce with a weakness on her left side, which progressed as the tumor redeveloped. According to Joyce's sister, following the operation Joyce refused to use a walker or even admit that her disabling condition was worsening. Although her sister wanted her to have round-the-clock care, Joyce only agreed to have someone in the apartment in the mornings. One night she tried to walk to the bathroom without the aid of her walker. After taking only a few steps she fell on the floor and was too weak to stand or crawl back to her bed where the phone was located. All night she screamed for help, but no one heard. When the home-care worker came in at 8:00 A.M. for her five-hour shift, she found Joyce whimpering on the floor. At that point, her sister insisted that she have twenty-four-hour-a-day care. Reluctantly, Joyce agreed.

She acknowledged the cancer was spreading and began looking for "miracle" cures. When a radiologist and another surgeon offered to perform an experimental procedure with a minimal possibility of success, Joyce jumped at the opportunity. It wasn't successful and left her with total paralysis on her left side. It became clear the tumor was rapidly growing, and the surgeon told her nothing could be done to slow it down. Although her sister tried to place her in a hospice facility, she was told the waiting lists were too long. That suited Joyce, who insisted that if she was going to die—something she still wasn't convinced about—she wanted to die at home.

The first time I met Joyce was one week after she began hospice home service. The home health-care worker asked me to wait in the living room until she dressed her. The furniture was simple and well-worn; probably bought in the 1960s. The walls were covered with pictures of a young, attractive woman full of joy. In each of them was a large muscular man with tattoos covering both arms. While she was smiling in every picture with her arm around him and her head tilted toward his, he never smiled nor showed any visible affection toward her.

"You can come in now," the health-care worker said as she opened the door to the bedroom.

Pictures similar to those in the living room covered the bedroom walls. Joyce was propped up and stared straight ahead at a large TV. She was the same woman in the pictures, but older and lacking the joy I saw in them. She was wearing a green bathrobe with "You're the one" embroidered all over it in red. Her hair was done in a bouffant, almost matching the pictures in the living room, and she had on a great deal of makeup. When I said hello, she barely glanced at me, nodding her head and continuing to look forward at the TV that was tuned to a game show. I sat down next to her and didn't say anything. For five minutes she stared at the TV and then, still not looking at me, began speaking.

"You probably know, they've given me six months. But I don't believe them."

"Why is that?" I asked.

"Well, for one thing, I feel as if the medicine I'm taking, along with the effects of the radiation, is still working. As long as I'm breathing, there's still hope."

I nodded my head. According to Joyce's sister, she was told that the effect of the radiation had reached its zenith and the accompanying drugs were not retarding the tumor's growth. Before receiving hospice care, she signed a document acknowledging that she had six months or less to live. I've found signing documents doesn't always lead to acceptance. People can't be forced to accept they are dying before they're ready. I didn't think Joyce was close, despite the deterioration of her body.

"Exactly what is it that you do?" she said.

It was a reasonable question, since the range of possible activities is broad. Most terminally ill people who were offered a hospice volunteer by an agency had little idea what we did.

"I don't administer medicine or do housecleaning. Beyond that, almost anything."

"I'm not interested in what you don't do. Tell me what you will do," she said, sounding annoyed.

"Well, that depends upon you."

"What depends upon me?"

"What your needs are. I can sit, we can talk, I can run errands. Your choice. Just ask me and I'll let you know if I can do it."

"How about changing the channel on the TV?"

"I think I can do that."

"Can't miss my soaps."

I walked to the TV and turned it to the channel she wanted. As I returned to my chair, I noticed that the remote control was within reach of her good hand. As she intently watched the drama unfolding, I glanced around the room at the photographs. Most were taken outdoors, and judging by the style of clothing and the change in Joyce's face, I guessed they were ten to fifteen years old. The contrast between Joyce's expressions and the man's was startling—almost as if they were asked to pose with opposite emotions. On every photograph he appeared to be alert to something that the camera lens couldn't see, while she appeared "dreamy." I kept looking for something that could differentiate the photographs: aging, more or less affection, a difference in expression. But nothing other than the settings and clothes changed. It appeared as if two manikins were moved around the country and photographed. Occasionally, I looked back at the TV, hoping she wouldn't notice I was staring at the photographs. During the entire hour, she never said anything, or even looked at me. Since I usually try to keep my first visits short, I rose to leave.

"I'll have to leave now. Thanks for allowing me to visit. Would you like me to come back next week?" I said, preparing myself for a rejection.

"Well, of course," she said, sounding shocked I would even consider that she didn't want me to return.

I told her that if she wasn't up for a visit the following week to call the office. I've had patients who were too embarrassed to tell me in person that I wasn't wanted back. Sometimes it's just a bad match; other times a family member felt so uncomfortable with death, they preferred surrogates to provide comfort to their loved one. I didn't think that was the case with Joyce's sister.

I began visiting her once every week. For the first three weeks, I felt as if I was watching the layers of an onion being peeled. At first, she would reveal only the most superficial things about herself: where she went to high school, what her job was, her favorite movie, and so forth. Sometimes this kind of information is as personal as a hospice patient chooses to be. But then things changed. She started playing a game in which she would ask me something about my life, and if I answered, she would tell me something about her life. It was a nonsexual version of strip poker. There didn't seem to be many limits on what she wanted to know about me. I had been married to the same woman for thirty-five years and often wondered why she stayed with me. I had two grown children whom I loved, and they loved me, but I felt guilty about not being a better father. I was retired from the university and was delighted not to be there. I had cancer and didn't know how long I would live. My excessive sweating was due to the hormone treatments I was receiving.

Yes, cancer sucks. Yes, I missed the life I had before the cancer. Was I hopeful that the cancer would remain controlled?—I didn't know. Was I afraid of dying?—No, I didn't think so, but it was still too theoretical for me. There were other questions I wasn't comfortable answering and would diplomatically move her on to other topics. During the fourth week that I visited, she told me about her twenty-five-year involvement in a reading project for economically disadvantaged children, but she described her activities in a throwaway tone as if they were inconsequential.

During one visit Joyce asked me to answer the phone, since it was on the other side of the room. I heard an automated message from the phone company, which I assumed was just another one of the solicitation calls I routinely hung up on, until I heard, "You will be receiving a collect call from an inmate incarcerated in the California penal system. If you wish to block this call and any others coming from inmates, press one. If you wish to accept this call, press two."

As I turned to Joyce and was about to ask her what to do, she said, "Press two and please give me the phone."

I handed over the receiver, and as I left the room I heard, "Hi, babe, how're you doing?" Thirty minutes later she called for me.

I sat down next to her and waited for her to say something.

"Well, aren't you going to ask me about that call?"

"No."

"You're not interested?" she said, sounding disappointed.

"Would you like to tell me about it?"

"That all depends."

"On what?"

"Are you the type of person who makes value judgments?"

"Not anymore." She smiled.

"That was Bill. I met him at a bar fifteen years ago and we fell instantly in love. At least I did. We saw each other off and on until he was convicted of burglary and went to Folsom. I guess that was about twelve years ago. He got out, got back into trouble, and went back to prison. His sentence keeps getting extended. You know, it's so hard staying clean in there."

"It must be difficult for you."

"Yes, it is. We've planned a life together. But when it comes close to a release date, something always happens. And now this cancer thing. I haven't been able to visit him since it started, and he can only call me once a month." As she started crying, she reached out for my hand.

"I've lived my life within a dream. Without it my life would have been a piece of crap."

She wept while I continued to hold her hand. Over the next month, I learned more about Joyce and her relationship with Bill—most of it had taken place while he was incarcerated. The calls kept coming—some from other inmates asking for money. I informed the hospice agency after the first phone call, then immediately contacted Joyce's sister. The inmates were always contrite and tried to sound genuinely concerned about Joyce, but there was a woman who kept calling with a transparent agenda. Once when Joyce was sleeping and I wouldn't wake her, she insisted on making her plea to me.

"I'm so worried about Bill," she said. "When Joyce dies who will take care of him? He'll need money when he gets out, and without Joyce there won't be anyone."

"I'll let Joyce know you called."

"Are you sure you can't wake her? I know she'll want to talk to me."

"No, I don't think so. She's just taken some medication and she's sleeping soundly."

"But can't you just wake—"

"I'll tell her you called," I said, hanging up the phone before I could be badgered again.

The woman's calls continued and were usually frantic. There was always something about Bill needing money. The calls I heard—Joyce no longer asked me to leave her room—

clearly indicated that these people, both in jail and outside, were more interested in her money than her health. Most of the conversations had to do with her will. She told me she was leaving some money to Bill, but everything else would go to her sister and her sister's children. The woman wanted her to change the will, leaving a larger amount to Bill.

As the weeks continued and Joyce's lucidity declined, the calls became more frequent. By then Joyce's sister had assumed her power of attorney. Although Joyce had agreed to that, she pleaded not to block calls from Bill, other inmates, or the woman. As painful as it was, her sister allowed the calls to continue. All of the caretakers and I were to accept the calls but never wake Joyce to take them, and if we saw the call was upsetting her, try to end it.

"They're my life—everything that connects me to what's still important," I heard her say to her sister.

There were pleas from friends of Bill who needed "just fifty dollars to get enough for cigarettes from the canteen." Others were from the woman, who began accusing me of not allowing her to speak with Joyce.

"As long as I have hope I might live, a life with Bill is possible when he gets out of jail," Joyce said.

On one visit she looked at a phone message taken by a caretaker when she was sleeping. After reading it, she handed it to me. It was from someone named Johnny who was asking her to send money to him in prison. By the content of the message, it sounded like this wasn't the first time he asked.

"You know, Johnny never gets enough money from his family for even a pack of smokes. I like sending him and some of the other boys a little for their needs. Could you get my checkbook? It's over there in the dresser."

I retrieved it and gave it to Joyce. Her sister told me that I should allow her to write the checks and just give them to her. If they were reasonable, she would forward them. If not, she wouldn't.

"Jeez, my mind isn't so good today. I forget Johnny's number. Could you look through that box in the hall closet and find it?"

Joyce explained to me that checks couldn't be sent directly to prisoners; they had to be sent to a special prison account with the inmate's number written on it. The storage box was filled to the top with what appeared to be legal documents and hundreds of receipts. I couldn't help reading them as I tried to find Johnny's number. Joyce had typed in the particulars on boilerplate loan forms. They were conditions such as "I promise to enroll in treatment," "I will not drink anymore," "I will stop using cocaine," and "I will not come into Joyce's apartment without permission." Some were for amounts as low as $50, while a few were for $10,000. The documents and money order receipts went back fifteen years. Only three small loans had "paid in full" written on them. A few indicated small portions were repaid, such as $50 on a $1,000 loan, or $5 on a $50 loan. I eventually found Johnny's number in a stack of twenty Western Union receipts, each for $50, the amount I later learned was the maximum that could be sent each month. I gave her Johnny's number and watched her try to write the check. With the tumor growing, her right arm was now affected.

"Stan, could you do it for me?" I did and hoped her sister would tear it up.

Not all of the calls were negative. There were ones from people she helped years ago in the reading program. During one of my visits, there were five of those calls. Fortunately, Joyce was alert enough that day to receive them. Although I couldn't hear the conversations, I could hear Joyce's responses.

"Thank you. It was a pleasure working with you."

"I'm so happy you are doing well."

"Imagine, you're a college graduate!"

What I found confusing was that even though everyone was expressing appreciation for what she did for them, she didn't act as if it was important.

"Stan," she said on one visit, "could you print out my e-mails? Someone said that they sent something they want me to read."

I went to her computer and accessed her e-mail account. Her health problems had become known at the reading center and her e-mail address was disseminated to her past students. I counted more than 150 unread e-mails from people she had helped in the past. I printed all of them and took them to her bedside.

"Joyce, here are e-mails from the people you helped. Would you like me to read them to you?" By then she was having difficulty with her vision.

"I guess so," she said with the same emotion she might have displayed if I asked her if she wanted to hear the latest weather report.

Dear Ms. Joyce,

You may not remember me, but I was that kid who never smiled. The guy who would refuse to even look at you when we read together. You probably thought I didn't appreciate what you did, but that's not true. You were the first person who took an interest in me. You never wanted anything or unlike other people, including my parents, never told me what a rotten person I was. You just patiently showed me how to read. I became a reading specialist because of you. Your kindness transformed me and now, whenever I sit next to a child who has problems reading I think of you and know what I'm doing is important and I hope as life-changing as what you did for me. I can't thank you enough for giving me a life.

The e-mail was difficult for me to read. As a teacher, this was the type of feedback I craved but only sparingly received. Who wouldn't be moved, to see that something you did a long time ago not only helped someone then but also was instrumental in shaping other lives in the present? It was like dropping a stone into a pond and watching the beautiful ripples as they kept moving outward. And here was Joyce, receiving not one but scores of similar e-mails. When I finished reading the e-mail, I looked at her and didn't see any reaction. At first, I thought her medication was affecting her awareness. How could anyone not respond to this incredible message?

"Would you like me to read another one?"

"No. Put them over there on the table."

Her words were quick and her reaction had nothing to do with her medication. And asking that they be placed in a spot where she couldn't look at them meant these weren't important.

"Has Bill called today?" she said when I returned to her bedside.

"No, there weren't any phone calls."

"Are you sure? He was upset a few days ago. You know, they're allowing him extra calls because I'm so sick. They'll probably stop when I get better."

"What was he upset about?"

"When he called, he asked me if I had changed the will. I told him that I couldn't do anything like that because my sister was now signing everything. God, he became so angry! He kept saying 'What about me? What about me?' I accused him of just wanting my money, but he said no. He said that without the money he couldn't hire a lawyer who could get him out early so we could be together. I didn't believe him, so I hung up."

We both sat quietly. I didn't know what Joyce was thinking. It was clear to me that Bill and his inmate buddies were only concerned about her money. I felt they would do or say anything to get it. Prior to Joyce's last phone call to Bill, none of the people who were calling knew Joyce's sister had been given her power of attorney. In prior weeks she had told me that what sustained her all these years was the dream she had of being with Bill when he got out of prison. There was still hope, in her mind, that the cancer might go into remission.

And even if she remained paralyzed on one side, she could get used to a wheelchair.

"Could you imagine, Bill pushing me around the ranch?" She laughed. No, I couldn't imagine the man in those pictures doing anything kind. "I realized Bill still loves me. His anger didn't have anything to do with money." I nodded, doing everything I could not to become someone who "makes judgments."

By my next visit her periods of lucidity were diminishing. During a four-hour stay she was conscious for only thirty minutes. And often she would hallucinate, either about things that were occurring in the room or believing she was somewhere else. The side rails on her bed became the bars on a cell. The movement by the aide in the kitchen was a gang of people who had taken over her apartment. The apartment really wasn't an apartment, but the ranch she and Bill bought when he got out of jail. With the tumor growing, it became more difficult to convince her that what she was experiencing wasn't real. At first I could bring her back to reality through simple logic.

"Joyce, do you see that picture on the wall?"

"Yes," she said between wails.

"Where is that picture?" Joyce ignored me, whimpering with a frightened look. "Joyce," I said louder. "Where is that picture?"

"In my apartment," she said.

"If it's in your apartment, then this can't be jail, right?" As her whimpering stopped I smiled and leaned back in the chair.

"Yes, yes. You're right," she said as the frightening image vanished for her.

But eventually, the strategies stopped working and the panic she experienced could often only be controlled with narcotics. As she came closer to dying, many of her regrets about her life occupied a large portion of her lucid hours. As her body began winding down, she no longer denied that she was dying. And that realization was frightening.

"I'm dying, aren't I?" she said.

"Why do you think that?"

"Nothing's working anymore. And inside, I know. I just know."

"Is there anything I can do for you to make this time easier?" She thought for a minute, and I could see tears forming.

"No. It's too late. I've waited my whole life for him. None of the dreams we had will happen. I'm going to die, and he'll have no one. I've wasted my entire life. I'll leave nothing behind."

I got up from my chair and went to the desk where the stack of e-mails had remained untouched. I sat back down and held the papers in front of her.

"Look at these," I said. Eventually she did look. "These are only some of the lives you've changed. Lives you probably saved, some who may have been destined for the same fate as Bill. You've made a difference. You've given these people a life. You have a legacy." I sat back in my chair, still holding her hand and waiting for her realize that her own life did count. The tears were flowing freely as she looked across the room at pictures of Bill and her.

"But my life with Bill. It won't happen." She closed her eyes and went to sleep.

During the next three weeks there were no more phone calls from inmates or the woman. Joyce began sleeping for longer periods of time, often waking in a panic, screaming, "Where am I?" or "They're coming," or other words that were just as disturbing to hear. Sometimes her sister or I could convince her that she was safe since we were next to her. When that and medication didn't help, we held her hand and waited for the panic to stop. I never felt that Joyce had relief from her terrifying images. A few days before she died, she tried sorting out her life, as I had seen many do as they came closer to dying. For most, the deliberations were similar to the movement of a child's seesaw. On one side were accomplishments and the positive things they had done throughout their lives. On the other side were unfulfilled dreams and regrets. Spirituality, regardless of the form it took, was always a big element on the positive side, but not necessarily an overriding factor. Regrets, unfinished business, and unfulfilled dreams materialized as the overweight bully that could tilt the seesaw, forcing the positive things people had done in their lives to become irrelevant. For Joyce, her broken dreams about life with Bill overshadowed even the effects of helping hundreds of children.

One day I arrived to find that Joyce was actively dying. Her sister was at her side. Even though Joyce wasn't conscious, we talked to her about those parts of her life her sister felt were positive. We took turns reading the e-mails from the people she helped. By then, the stack had grown to more than 250, each one expressing gratitude. For two hours we read, not knowing if she could hear us.

What Joyce wanted most, she couldn't have. There probably would never have been a life with Bill, even if he hadn't been in jail. According to her sister, when Bill wasn't incarcerated he would constantly scam Joyce out of money and occasionally become violent. When he was in jail, the abuse was replaced with manipulation. If he didn't need money, his fellow inmates did, or the woman who kept calling needed it for an attorney who could get Bill and her son out of jail.

More than five hundred people were at the memorial service for Joyce after she died. Most were the people Joyce helped when she volunteered and many brought their families.

"Why are we here, Daddy?" I heard one child ask her father.

"We're honoring a very great woman. She was the one who taught me to read. Without her, I don't know what I would have become."

As I listened to him and others as they eulogized Joyce, I was troubled knowing she hadn't been able to recognize the good things in her life as a way to overcome her pain. She had placed fifteen years of her life on hold for a dream that didn't pan out. I realized I had done something similar after my first series of hormone injections. My surgeon started the injections one month after my prostate was removed. I would have them every three months for eighteen months. If after eighteen months the PSA was undetectable, we would stop until it rose. I was ecstatic when the first series of injections ended, knowing the hot flashes, lack of sexual arousal, low energy, and moodiness would stop within a few months. Unfortunately, the conversion of muscle to fat and the bone loss that made me vulnerable to fractures were permanent. With each three-month checkup and no detection of PSA, I began believing the cancer cells might have been killed, despite my surgeon repeatedly telling me they weren't.

For the next eighteen months, my hope grew. But as it did, I moved further away from enjoying life minute by minute. From the time of the first injection I had resolved to treat every day as if it was my last. Common experiences attained an exquisite level of delight: listening to a moving piece of music, walking on the beach, even the simple act of petting my dog. I chose my words carefully then, especially when I needed to give critical comments to student clinicians. My interaction with my wife and children benefited the most. I became more caring and never hesitated in telling them how much I loved them and appreciated everything they were doing for me. But a strange thing happened as I approached the eighteen-month "no detection" period—my hope that I beat the cancer brushed away my new life as easily as a broom whisks aside dust. I was comfortable living with "hope" until I received a call from my surgeon.

"The results of the blood test just came in. I'm sorry but your PSA is rising. We need to restart the hormone injections next week."

Poof! Not only did hope disappear, but as I looked back on who I became during the intervening time between the onset of hope and learning that my dream wasn't going to be fulfilled, it wasn't pleasant realizing that I had allowed hope to let the new me slip away. People often contrast hope with hopelessness, as if the former is always positive and the latter always negative. It's a false dichotomy based on a simplistic understanding of the role of hope. For Joyce, hope prevented her from living in the present and appreciating the marvelous things she had accomplished. For me, hope transformed the scientist and humanist in me into someone who put all faith on the throw of the dice. Worse, for eighteen months it robbed me of being more genuine with the people I loved.

The absence of hope isn't a negative state. The disappearance of hope put me squarely into the present, since I know I can die at anytime (although with prostate cancer I'll have some warning). Given all I know about prostate cancer and my abominable lack of "luck," it makes sense to do everything as if today is my last day. Stephen Levine, in his book *A Year to Live,** poses the question: what would you do if you knew you had one year to live? I read it shortly after the removal of my prostate, when my prognosis was uncertain. One year seemed like a long time then. As months passed, the insights I gained from the book slowly dissolved as the possibility of dying drifted away from my thinking and hope became stronger. After the second round of hormone injections, however, I listened even more closely to my hospice patients. I watched an intensity of living in everything they did, from greeting me to pondering what they had done with their life, to savoring a spoonful of ice cream. I no longer invest energy in hoping that the cancer will remain under control—I'm too busy living.

* Stephen Levine, *A Year to Live: How to Live This Year As If It Were Your Last* (New York: Harmony/Bell Tower, 1997).

7

Undifferentiated Love

> The spiritual journey involves going beyond hope and fear, stepping into unknown territory, continually moving forward. The most important aspect of being on the spiritual path may be to just keep moving.
>
> —Pema Chödrön

"We're going to ask you to fall in love with people who'll leave you within months or even weeks." The trainer paused for the words to sink in before he continued. "Then we're going to ask you to do it again and again."

That was the first day of my volunteer training session five years ago at the Zen Hospice Project. I wondered how it would be possible to allow myself to fall in love with someone, knowing, with certainty, they would be leaving me within a very short period of time. Would I have permitted myself to fall in love with my wife of thirty-five years if I knew she would die shortly after our first meeting? Most likely, I would have pulled back, despite the intense feeling of love I had knowing her for only a few hours. But here was someone asking me to do it, not once, but repeatedly. And I did.

For five years I fell in love with the hospice patients I spent time with, at least most of them, and mindful of Thich Nhat Hanh's admonition to treat every person as if she or he was your mother, I tried smoothing their journey toward death. With some I was more successful than others. But when I left the bedside I knew I had done my best—and that was satisfying, whatever the outcome. But that abstract concept, just like so many abstract ideas I had before beginning hospice, was stood on its head when I met Andrea. She had been described to me as a "difficult" case.

Because of my thirty years' experience and training as a speech-language pathologist, I usually was assigned to cases such as these ones that required counseling skills, which I relished. Andrea had breast cancer and was two years younger than I. The "difficulty," I was told, involved a personality conflict between Andrea's brother, Eliot, who had been caring for her for three months, and hospice staff who visited them in Andrea's apartment. With past patients, I rarely witnessed any friction. They and their families were usually grateful that people willingly ministered to them as they approached death. When I arrived at Andrea's apartment, Eliot asked me to wait in the kitchen while he helped get Andrea into the bathroom. As I waited I looked around the room and saw pictures of well-known musicians from the worlds of classical, bluegrass, blues, and jazz. Andrea not only had pictures of people I idolized, but each was signed with an inscription that went well beyond the usual words you find on autographed photographs. I was still gawking at them when Eliot came back into the kitchen.

"She's a gifted musician, you know. She played with all of them," Eliot said, gesturing to the pictures.

"What instrument?"

"Woodwinds, mostly. Flute, piccolo, clarinet, and some from third-world countries." He sat down on Andrea's motorized wheelchair and eyed me for a few moments before speaking. "I did ask for a volunteer, but now I'm not sure I want one."

"Would you like me to leave?" I said.

"Not yet. I'll let Andrea make that decision."

From the bathroom I heard a noise that sounded like a combination of retching and crying. Eliot lowered his head and slowly shook it back and forth. When he raised it, his eyes were filled with tears.

"It's so messed up. She's allergic to every painkiller that can help. She's dying, and there's nothing I can do to make it easier. I can't tell you how hard it is to see my younger sister in pain."

"You're right," I said.

"About what?" he said, as if I had just challenged him.

"I can't know what you're feeling. I can't imagine what it must be like to be with someone you love and know there's nothing that can stop the pain. And worse, not knowing when it will end for both of you." Eliot looked at me without saying anything and we both listened to Andrea.

"She had a mastectomy three years ago. We all thought the cancer was gone and Andrea could get on with her life. Then six months ago it came back, like a fucking train." Eliot looked at me, as if waiting for a reaction to his words. "I came to stay with her three months ago when she couldn't take care of herself. She hardly eats anymore. I think it was about a month ago when she started eating only a few bites of whatever I made for her. Then just when I thought her end would be easier, she now can only take in liquids. Her life was just coming together again after the mastectomy."

I heard three taps from a stick hitting a wall.

"I'll take her back to her room and get her ready," Eliot said. As he was about to leave the kitchen, he paused, and turning to me, said, "I think you'll do, but we'll see." Fifteen minutes later he returned. "You can go in now. I'll stay out here. Andrea wants to meet you alone. But I just want you to know," he said, as if he was a mother hen hovering over a chick with a hawk circling above, "I'll be right out here."

Andrea was sitting upright in her bed, leaning against a headboard that was hand-painted with pictures of children. The room was cluttered with books, pictures, and a variety of musical instrument cases. A loose-fitting flannel shirt draped over her, and she was wearing fleece warm-up pants. Her feet were pulled up near her knees, in a posture that reminded me of my daughter when she was a child and I would come into her room at night to read her a story. But even Andrea's crunched-up position couldn't hide the fact that she was probably at least six feet tall. Her blond hair, with the slightest bit of gray showing, ended at her waist. Neither the deterioration of her body nor her sunken cheeks hid her beauty.

"I'm so glad to have you here," she said, barely above a whisper.

I sat down next to her before speaking. "Thank you for allowing me to visit," I said, then waited for her to speak.

"I finally felt whole again, and I have so much love to give, but nobody to give it too." As she began crying, I reached out for her hand and held it. Hospice patients have often shared intimate thoughts with me, but never this quickly.

"And look what I'm doing to my brother. He's been here for three months. I can't do anything by myself anymore. He doesn't deserve this."

I didn't try to comfort her with words. There weren't any, at least none I found useful. I continued holding her hand as we sat looking at each other, both of us silent, both comfortable just being in each other's presence. I couldn't understand what I was feeling toward her, but it was an attraction that made me uncomfortable. There didn't seem to be anything sexual about it. If there was, it was probably something I could just chalk it up to the rise and fall of hormones from the cancer treatment. But what I felt seemed far beyond anything physical, and the feeling was so unique to me that it was frightening. Eventually she spoke.

"Tell me about yourself," she said. I began telling her about my family, my interests, that I had been a hospice volunteer for five years, and other biographical information. She interrupted me and said, "No, tell me about *you*." When I hesitated, she said, "I need to know the type of person you are."

I've never been reluctant to be honest with hospice patients. I had often been told that there is a professional line which volunteers shouldn't cross. It's a line that keeps an appropriate distance between the person who is dying and someone who is there to be a companion. The expression most often used about maintaining this line in the context of the helping professions is "boundaries." In general, the emphasis on establishing boundaries is good advice. For one thing, as volunteers are cautioned, being drawn too much into other people's lives can cause you to lose perspective and suffer burnout.

But I've never been very good with establishing boundaries in my personal life, and in hospice I never experienced burnout. The loss I always felt with each person's death was more than compensated by the richness of our interactions and by the honor of being involved in poignant moments common in the dying experience but generally avoided in everyday life. In many situations I did cross the boundary from ancillary health worker to friend. Opening or redefining the boundaries enabled me to be more effective and also allowed me to learn many lessons. With that history, I saw no reason to stop Andrea from pulling me across the boundary with her questions. Was I satisfied with my life? What did I regret? Was I afraid of dying? What would I have done if my wife developed breast cancer?

Within a few minutes, I was talking about issues I never shared with anyone, answering questions no one had ever asked me. With each answer I gave, she quickly reciprocated. It was almost as if my honesty was the lubricant for her talking about her feelings. I know that in some psychological approaches there's a technique whereby, in showing the client that you're vulnerable, they in turn show their vulnerability. But that's not what happened as I spoke with Andrea. I was never calculating about the things I said to a person in hospice, and with Andrea I found myself talking as if we had known each other our entire lives, as if we were two halves of the same person. We talked about our values, about what we wanted from life: in Andrea's case, what she would certainly never get, and in my case, what I probably wouldn't get. After a while, she asked if I could help her sit up, changing position to reduce the pain. I helped her to the edge of the bed, and she rocked back and forth. She abruptly stopped and looked down to the floor.

"Great boots," she said, pointing to a pair of new lizard-skin cowboy boots I was wearing.

"Thanks. I used to wear them all the time, but I had to stop when I developed hip problems. I was in Tucson last week delivering a lecture and I got this urge to see if I could wear boots again. I hoped to wear them to a very formal wedding in October, but both my wife and daughter said that I needed to wear regular black shoes."

She looked straight at me and leaned forward. "No, trust me, you need to wear them."

I didn't know what to make of her insistence that I wear the boots. But just like other things that happened in hospice that I didn't understand, I tucked this exchange away in my mind—although not without first quickly thinking how I would explain to Wendy and Jessica that I would be wearing those boots, even if they might be socially inappropriate. I looked at the wall clock and realized I had been there for almost three hours. Andrea was tiring and I was feeling . . . actually, I'm not sure what I was feeling. Maybe what a hiker might experience walking along a precipice with a thousand-foot drop on one side and a flat surface on the other side. You're inches away from tragedy, yet exhilarated by walking on the edge.

"I have to go now," I said.

"Thank you for coming. This has been very good for me."

"And for me too. Thank you for allowing me to visit.

"I feel we've known each other for a long time," she said.

I nodded in agreement. "I think we could have been great friends if we knew each other earlier."

"I know we could have. Will you come back again?" Andrea asked.

"I thought you'd never ask. I'm leaving tomorrow for a trip, but I'll be back next Tuesday." She nodded her head.

"Where are you going?"

"New Orleans."

"Jazz Fest?"

"Yes."

It was the broadest smile I had seen since I arrived. I rose and went to kiss her goodbye on the cheek. As we embraced I felt an energy I never experienced before. It wasn't sexual, nor the feeling you have when you embrace a friend you haven't seen for a while, or say goodbye to someone you'll miss terribly. I didn't know what it was, but as I was leaving her room, I said, "I'll give Eliot my cell phone number. If you feel you need to talk, have him call me. Any time of the day or night. Anytime."

Again, a violation of a rule—don't give your telephone number to patients. Hospice patients and families are told to call the office if they need to contact anyone. It wasn't the first time I had given out my number. In the past, I would provide it if I felt the person or family needed an assurance of support—something they could hold on to, sort of like a child's security blanket. Nobody ever called. But I knew that having a way to reach a hospice volunteer, just in case someone needed to talk, was helpful to people. Whether or not they ever used the number, giving it to them was a gesture that said, "I'm here for you." This was the first time I wanted to receive a call.

I left the next day for Jazz Fest, where I would meet friends who also shared a passion for music. As I listened to incredible groups, an image surfaced in my mind, of Andrea sitting on her bed saying she was ready to give love but there was nobody to accept it. I really didn't know what I was feeling about her. She was beautiful, talented, and insightful. As I watched each act at Jazz Fest, I imagined Andrea on the stage playing, joking with the legends; some of the musicians were among those who had signed pictures of themselves and now covered her walls. I kept looking at my cell phone. Maybe she had called and I couldn't hear because of the loud music? I must have pulled the phone out of my pocket three or four times an hour. I even thought of calling Eliot, just to see how things were going. I knew that was definitely beyond the boundaries. For me to call meant that I had shifted my focus from her needs to my own. No, if Andrea needed to speak with me, she would have had Eliot call. At night when I went to bed I left the cell phone next to me, and I explained to my friend who was sharing the hotel room that I might be receiving a call at any time. Since I had told him about Andrea, he said he understood. Maybe he did, but I didn't.

I wondered if I was obsessing about her in a way that wouldn't help her death. There didn't seem to be anything sexual in my attraction. Nor did I seem to be experiencing rescue fantasies, where excessive altruism takes over a helping relationship. No, I felt as if this was something very different. I was moving down an unfamiliar path. In the past, I had been pulled along some new path by my interaction with a hospice patient, but none of those journeys were ever frightening. Maybe a little uncomfortable, as with any venture in developing self-awareness. But this occasion with Andrea was different. I was feeling something for her that went well beyond what I had experienced with any other patient.

I returned on a Monday night and went to see Andrea on Tuesday morning. At the front door of the apartment, Eliot told me she was weaker and barely able to speak. I entered her room, we embraced, and then I sat next to her.

"I missed you," she said in a barely audible voice.

"And I missed you. I meant it when I said you could call."

"I wanted to, but I couldn't talk," she whispered. "Anyway, you were at Jazz Fest. I wouldn't interrupt that. I know how exciting it is."

"You've been there?"

"Yes, I played there."

She pointed to a picture I hadn't noticed before, on the far wall of the bedroom, and motioned for me to look at it. There she was, playing a flute on the same stage I was in front of when I kept hoping she would call.

"I need to use the commode. Could you have Eliot come in?"

"Sure." I called Eliot and waited in the next room. The space contained a jumble of objects that probably had once been in the bedroom before they were cleared out to make room for the oxygen tanks and pump. On the floor was a blue gas tank from a Triumph motorcycle. In the corner was a pair of purple cowboy boots, arranged in such a way as to give the impression that these objects were more important than anything else in the room. On the shelf were a number of books that caught my interest because so many of them were ones I also owned. But the most striking object was a four-foot-wide by six-foot-tall painting on the wall. In the center was a naked woman, her breasts covered with a translucent cloth, running through a consuming fire, her blond hair trailing behind her. Most riveting was the expression on her face. I can't describe it, other than to say it was what someone might look like if in one single expression they tried conveying anger, horror, pain, sorrow, and longing. I don't know how long I stared at it before I realized that Eliot was standing behind me.

"She's also a painter."

Neither of us said anything as we stood looking at the painting until we heard the tapping of a stick from the bedroom. Eliot left, and I remained looking at the painting.

"She's ready," Eliot said when he came back.

I went back into the bedroom, where Andrea was sitting on the side of the bed. She motioned for me to hand her a popsicle stick with a small sponge attached to the end of it. I dipped it into a glass of water and sat on the side of the bed watching as she sucked on it as if it was a delicious morsel from a five-star restaurant. As pain coursed through her body, she leaned on me and I held her. She no longer had the strength to cry out in pain; she could only grimace and tightly hold my hand until it subsided fifteen minutes later. I helped her lie back onto the bed, and she moved to her side so she could face me.

"Thank you," she mouthed, but no sound came out. She picked up a pen and a pad and wrote, *Tell me a story.*

"True or fiction?" I asked.

She shrugged her shoulders. In the past, there had been patients who knew I was a writer and who asked me to tell them a story. If I tried to read one, I usually was told no, no reading. They wanted to hear me say the words, looking directly at them.

"I saw your Triumph gas tank. Was that going to be part of something artistic?"

She shook her head no, and wrote, *Off my bike*.

My startled facial reaction made her grimace.

Think I'm making that up? she wrote.

"No, it's just like so many things in our lives, we've been on similar paths. I rode Triumph motorcycles for five years. That blue was the color of my last bike."

She reached out and grabbed my hand and gestured that I should now start the story. It would be a true one. One that spanned the years of my youth when the concerns for safety and propriety weren't even on the horizon of my thinking. As I moved through each episode, she would nod her head and point to herself. Grabbing the pen she wrote, *Me too! Me too!* From motorcycle adventures I moved back to my childhood. Our lives had been in tandem since we were children. Although there were vast differences between me growing up in a small town behind a grocery store and she being moved around the country by a military father, what each of us experienced in these disparate situations was uncannily similar.

I began understanding our connection. It was spiritual. Not some new-age notion of being part of the cosmic whole—that was too "loosey-goosey" for me. Not even the Buddhist idea of a collective consciousness—which had always been very abstract. This was something I could feel and also see in real-life vignettes. We were connected. If not, how was it possible that we had so many similar experiences and feelings, yet only knew each other for one week? There are no coincidences in life.

"Remember when you said that you had so much love to give and nobody to give it to?" She nodded her head yes. "You realize that wasn't true, don't you?" She nodded her head again and reached out for my hand, then after a few moments released it and picked up the pen.

Afraid dying? she wrote.

"I don't think so."

We met so I could help on other side?

It took me a while to answer. "I don't know. But what I do know is you've found someone to give your love to, and I've been able to get in touch with parts of myself I've hidden from everyone." She smiled, and still holding my hand she went to sleep.

The pain never stopped, but eventually our conversations did. By the third week, she no longer had the strength to write, and I didn't know if she was even aware of my presence. I would play my flute for her, continually joking that I couldn't play looking at the picture of her on the wall performing at Jazz Fest. At other times, I would tell her stories, some of which I made up on the spot, others that I wrote years ago. I hoped they helped, but I never could be sure. Even the most suspenseful story of European intrigue wasn't a match for the cancer. She would follow the story for a few minutes, then her face changed. It appeared she was focusing on my words as a way to combat the pain.

After a particularly difficult visit, Wendy asked me if I had fallen in love with Andrea. I immediately said, "No! That's absurd!" Wendy didn't mention it again. But afterward, as I thought back and realized how defensive my answer had been, I wondered if I had fallen in love with Andrea in more than a platonic sense. Was I envisioning her as someone I would want to have a relationship with? Even someone I would be willing to leave Wendy for? Was Andrea the female version of Sid, whom I had craved to have as a lifelong friend, despite knowing he would be dying within days? Possibly all the admonitions I had received and cavalierly disregarded about keeping boundaries tightly controlled contained more wisdom than I had given them credit for. And just possibly, the only reason I hadn't experienced this problem sooner had more to do with the type of people I cared for rather than any flaw in the warning.

Three weeks after Andrea died, I was able to begin answering these questions. The first thing I needed to do was understand what I felt for her. I had never been very good at describing emotions. What was pain? What was joy? What was love or a host of other "squishy" feelings? In many ways I viewed these in the same way that a Supreme Court justice answered the question "What is pornography?" He said, "I can't define it, but I know it when I see it." Yes, I had felt all of these emotions. Maybe I couldn't describe them—but I knew them when I felt them. What I felt for Andrea was definitely a form of love, but unlike anything I had ever experienced. As I thought about it, I realized that, for me, I needed to think about love as not being on a continuum, but rather as elements of a palette. The love I felt for Wendy, my children, my friends, even my flute, were different from what I felt for Andrea. None were better than any other. They were just different. Each type of love was unique, coming to me with differing conditions and consequences. With Andrea, the love I felt involved caring without receiving anything in return, and realizing that I was deeply connected to another person. We were, for lack of a better term, soul mates. I didn't wear the boots to the wedding. But in explaining why I wanted to, Wendy and I finally talked about my feelings toward Andrea. It was a discussion that brought us closer. Who would have thought that cowboy boots could have done that?

8

Forgiving

Forgiveness does not change the past,
but it does enlarge the future.

—Paul Boese

I was never very good at forgiving others. After all, why should I forgive someone, when I knew that I was absolutely right and they were absolutely wrong? Before the cancer, I thought I was right most of the time. I had a set of values that governed my behaviors. Nothing very complicated or profound. Just the ordinary ones like, be kind, do unto others as you would like them to do unto you. Those types of implicit rules. Maybe a little more sophisticated than the Ten Commandments, but similar. My problem was in assuming that everyone should believe what I believed. That everyone should act as I acted. Arrogant? Absolutely! But even worse (for me), it became the basis for unending disappointment. When I felt people weren't meeting my expectations—when I knew they could do something different—I became indignant, refusing to accept behaviors different from what I would have done. I couldn't forgive them. A hospice patient named Ned led me to understand my folly.

Ned was at Maitri, a revered hospice facility in San Francisco for people with AIDS. Hospice By The Bay, as a contracting agency, provided Maitri with a full range of services. When I met Ned he was in a dining room trying to eat lunch. He was wearing a bib to prevent the food from falling onto his pajamas. I could see that it wasn't working. He was fifty-three, he had long, straight hair, and he was very thin. His file indicated that he probably had only a month to live, since the virus had moved to his brain.

"Hi Ned, I'm Stan." He slowly looked up from his bowl of soup and smiled. "Would you like some help with that?" I gestured toward the bowl.

"I sure would," he said with a slur that clearly indicated the AIDS was affecting his motor control. "I've been trying to eat this stuff for thirty minutes."

I looked around the room and saw that every available person was helping patients with less control than Ned. As I fed him one small spoon of soup after another, I explained that I was a volunteer from Hospice By The Bay, and that they'd sent me because he had requested someone to visit him. Ned finished the soup and asked me to wheel him back to his room.

"My mouth is too sore to eat anything solid," he said over his shoulder as we moved along the corridor.

We went back into his room, and an attendant and I prepared to move Ned into bed. I had been told there were open lesions on his body, with a very virulent herpes infection near his underarm. The attendant and I both put on gloves and gently lifted Ned from the wheelchair into bed. He thanked us, and the attendant left to care for another patient. I sat down at his bedside and waited for him to regain his breath.

"Do you know what I miss the most?" he said after a few minutes. I shook my head no. "Surfing. I lived in Newport Beach for the last twenty-five years. I'd get up in the morning if I wasn't too wasted from the night before and head down to the beach. If the surf was just right, I'd go out. If not, I'd try to pick up an odd job or get wasted with friends. Life was so good then." He paused as he looked at old puncture wounds on his withered arms. "I guess that's how I got this AIDS thing. Do you surf?"

"No, I never had enough coordination."

"When I lost mine a few months ago, I came up here. I thought my family might be able to help me out. I got an ex-wife and a son living here in Sacramento."

By the look on his face, I believed they probably didn't offer him any help, but I didn't ask and he didn't volunteer any additional information about them. After peering off into space for a few minutes, he turned to me and smiled.

"How are the Giants doing?" he said.

"The baseball season is over, Ned."

"Really? I thought I heard them on the radio the other day."

It was December. He looked concerned, as if he had just realized that the virus was attacking his mind.

"I'd really like to know more about surfing," I said. "I watch them off Ocean Beach, but I can't tell why they wait on some waves and try to catch others."

His face lit up and his words flowed, cogent and informative. Without having to plug in his failing memory for specific facts, he relaxed. I was transported to Newport Beach and felt as if I was sitting with him on a surfboard as he described incoming waves and how to position myself to ride the next one. With his words, I began to understand his fascination with surfing. Riding a wave was totally engrossing, forcing you to concentrate on what was happening in the moment. If you dwelled in the past or daydreamed about the future, by the time you traveled back to the present, the wave was already inshore. We talked about many things for the next thirty minutes: he asked again how the San Francisco Giants were doing; he asked if I knew whether or not it was a good surf day, what day was it, what year it was. But nothing about his illness. I realized our conversation had exhausted him physically and exacerbated the dementia. He would forget what he was saying in the middle of a sentence, repeating himself verbatim.

"Are you coming back?" he asked. "I sure would like to have some company again, Bruce. No, that's not your name. What is it?"

"Stan."

"Stan. Right. I forget sometime. Would you come back?"

"Yes, of course."

"When?"

"Next week at the same time."

"Next week?"

"Yes."

"What day is it today?

"Tuesday."

"So you're coming back again?"

"Yes."

"When?"

"I'll be here next Tuesday at eleven-thirty so I can help you with your lunch."

"Tuesday? Is today Tuesday?"

"Yes," I said, going to the calendar on his wall and circling the following Tuesday. "I'll have the attendant cross out each day so you can see when I'll be here."

"She'll do that for me?"

"Yes. And anything else you need. Just ask."

I had a week to examine my prejudices: you know, those deep within you that you deny exist. Ones like how much compassion can you have for someone who brought about a tragedy on himself, living a life with no apparent purpose. It was the same type of mixed feeling I had when I passed an aggressive, seemingly able-bodied but homeless panhandler. They should take responsibility for their dilemma, I would think. They should be actively seeking work. They shouldn't be using, no less re-using, hypodermics filled with dope. I still couldn't accept values that differed from my own. Yet, here was a person who made no excuses for his lifestyle, and he was so genuinely nice, you had to feel compassion for him.

When I came back the following Tuesday, Ned was telling an attendant that it was a good day to surf and he wanted to know where his swimming trunks were. The attendant walked over to the window and looked out at the brilliant blue sky.

"Sorry, Ned, it's a lousy day. The winds are blowing at over thirty miles per hour and a storm front is coming in. Look over there," he said, pointing at a building across the street. "Can't you see the lightening out there toward Catalina Island?"

"Damn. And I was so ready to go out today."

Although I was standing next to him, Ned ignored me and fell asleep. I didn't have another appointment until late afternoon, so I decided to sit there and read in case he woke. I don't remember what I was reading that day, but whatever it was, I was transported to another realm. So when I heard Ned speaking to me, I was shocked.

"I think I'm dying," he said. I turned and saw he was looking straight at me and his eyes were wide open.

"Why do you think that?"

"I feel like I'm getting weaker. You know, like at the end of a wave when it comes ashore."

He was significantly weaker than the last time I saw him, and he had stopped taking both food and water. "Is there anything I can do for you to make you more comfortable?" He closed his eyes, and since I thought he was going back to sleep, I returned to my book. After a few minutes, he opened his eyes and looked at me.

"I don't want to die alone," he said, then waited for my response.

"Would you like me to be with you when it happens?"

He smiled and went back to sleep. When I left, I told the nurse and the volunteer coordinator at Hospice By The Bay of Ned's request. Both assured me that they would call me when the time came. We all knew it was getting close. I started visiting Ned every day, sometimes just for a few minutes, other times for hours. With each visit I could feel my prejudices lessening. On one visit he appeared to have rallied, and he greeted me with a big smile as I entered the room.

"Carl, I'm so glad you came," Ned said to me with his head still on his pillow. I could see that his eyes weren't focusing, and I had no idea who Carl was.

"It's me, Ned. It's Stan. You remember, from Hospice By The Bay?"

"I thought you wouldn't come back."

"I told you I would."

"I know it's been hard on you," he said, barely above a whisper.

"No, I enjoy coming to visit you."

"You were right telling me to leave."

"Ned, it's me, Stan, not Carl."

"I shouldn't have asked you to take me in."

I stopped insisting that I was Stan.

"I didn't have the right to ask anything of you. A father shouldn't do that to his son."

I didn't know what to say as he waited for me to respond. I knew that insisting I wasn't his son wouldn't make any sense. For one thing, given his level of delusion, he wouldn't believe it. And second, he needed his son, right there next to him. But did I have the right to assume that role? And what if his son or wife would visit? How would they respond to someone impersonating Carl? Or what if friends came, and Ned told them about a visit from a son he hadn't spoken to in years? There wasn't time to call and ask anyone what to do. Nor did my training or experiences provide me with the rock-solid guidance I wanted. I decided to forget about logic and allow my heart to decide.

"It was all right what you did, Dad," I said.

"No, it wasn't. I haven't seen you or your mom in twenty years, and here I am, asking you for a place to stay. Even asking you to care for me. You were right telling me to find some other place." As I struggled for the next thing to say, his eyes seemed to focus and he said, "I forgive you." Then, just as quickly as the delusion began, it ended in a peaceful look as he drifted off to sleep.

I left Maitri wondering if I had done the right thing. I remembered in my training it was emphasized that we were to be a companion to the dying. Sometimes in the past I found the boundaries too restrictive. But this was different. Was this a breach of standard hospice ethics? Worse, was I doing something that wasn't in Ned's best interest? For the next few days I struggled with it, knowing I needed to explain what I did to the volunteer coordinator. I had always been given wide latitude because of my training and experience in an allied health profession. But I may have gone too far this time. I had been stopping in to see Ned every few days. Usually they were short visits; during some, he was unconscious for the entire time. One Tuesday, I was scheduled to visit him in the afternoon. I was working in my office when the phone rang.

"Hi, Stan," the volunteer coordinator said. "Were you planning on visiting Ned today?"

"Yes, this afternoon at one." I thought this was a good opportunity to tell her what I did, but before I could say anything, she spoke.

"I just heard from his nurse at Maitri. He's begun to actively die. I thought you would want to know."

"I'll go there now," I said. As I was driving to Maitri, I realized that if I had been at the gym, as I originally intended, I wouldn't have been available for the coordinator's call.

When I arrived at Maitri, I found a woman sitting at his side, talking to him with tears cascading down her cheeks. She noticed me and wiped her eyes.

"Hi, I'm Ellen."

"I'm Stan. I'm a volunteer from Hospice By The Bay."

"I came as soon as I heard. I'm an old friend of Ned's. He and I used to pal around years ago before he lost himself in surfing. I guess in some ways our lives ran parallel to each other."

I saw the faint track marks on her arm, which she had tried hiding with makeup. Since Ned was in his early fifties, I assumed she was about the same age, but she had that appearance of someone who led a hard life.

"Is he dying now?" she asked. I nodded my head yes, and she began crying again. She rose from her chair and kissed him on his forehead, allowing her lips to linger. After sitting back down, she said, "You know, Ned led a very interesting life. He married young and had a child. I forgot his name."

"Carl."

"Carl, yes that's it. He was about four when Ned left them. By then he and a bunch of us were heavily into drugs. I stayed in San Francisco and eventually got cleaned up. Ned took up surfing in Southern California. He still did drugs there, but not as much as he did here. I'd occasionally go down south, and he came up here sometimes."

As she talked, she gently stroked his face.

"Every time he came here he'd try to see his wife and son. She always refused to let him see Carl. Each time he would become really upset. Sometimes he'd just go off into another room and cry. Other times, I thought he would OD on the heroin. Then, when Carl got older, I think it was when he was about twelve, she said she'd let him decide if he wanted to see Ned. Ned got on the phone and told Carl that he'd like to see him. There was a long silence, then Ned hung up the phone and left my apartment. I knew he was hurting, but he never told me what Carl said to him. That was the last time I know of that he tried to see Carl. He also stopped calling him any-more. That's why I couldn't believe it when Ned told me a few days ago that Carl came to visit. Ned said that when he knew he was sick, he asked Carl for help, but Carl refused. Then out of the blue, he comes here to see his father and asks for forgiveness. Ned said he told Carl that he forgave him for not taking him in. When Ned was telling me this, there was such a look on his face. I don't know how to describe it. Peaceful. maybe. Yeah, that's what it was. Peaceful, like on a baby's face. Were you here when he came?"

"No, I wasn't."

We both looked at Ned and saw his breathing had become shallower and his eyes were open and fixed. I thought Ellen was feeling uncomfortable. For some loved ones, the reality of seeing someone drift off into death is difficult. For them, there is nothing spiritual about the event.

"I have to leave now," she said. "I've been with him for the last two hours."

"Don't worry, I'll stay with him." She rose to leave. "You know, one of the last senses to go is hearing. Would you like me to leave the two of you alone, so you can say goodbye?"

She nodded yes, and I walked out of the room. I didn't think there was much time left. After twenty minutes Ellen came out and thanked me. She left and I went in, sat next to Ned, and held his hand. As I sat at the bedside, I heard piano music. It had to be coming from the old upright piano in the common area. Despite being out of tune, the notes were incredibly sweet. There was no virtuosity in the playing, no arpeggios, nothing complicated at all. I don't even remember the song. But the feeling was so pure and genuine that people who were ambulatory left their rooms to listen. As I walked out of Ned's room, through open doors I could see patients who were confined to their beds listening intently. Even if they had visitors, nobody spoke. Although attendants were moving between rooms, they seemed to linger in the hallway and when they entered a room, they didn't say anything. As I approached the common area, I saw Ellen weeping as she played.

When I went back into Ned's room, I saw his breathing had changed. It was shallow, and the spaces between breaths had increased. I held his hand and said, "I'm right here, Ned, just like I promised." From a prone position, he sat straight up and looked forward, his arms wrapping around me for an instant, and then he fell back down on the bed. The spaces between breaths continued to increase until there was no inhalation. An indescribable stillness occurred next. As I looked at Ned, I saw the peacefulness of someone I imagined had relinquished everything negative in his life.

I informed the Maitri nurse and Hospice By The Bay that Ned had died. As I sat with him, I thought back on our time together. I didn't know if, as he died, he thought I was his son, or whether he knew it was me, or whether he even realized someone was holding him. What I was certain about was the power of offering forgiveness, and decided, like Ned, to offer it.

For years I had been angry with some of my former university colleagues about the events that surrounded my retirement. I had been teaching, writing, and been involved in research projects while directing a university speech-language disorders program. When my sleep disorder had become acute, I had confided at a program meeting that I would no longer be able to do as many things as I had once done, things that benefited my colleagues and gave the program high visibility. If I were to remain at the university, some of my responsibilities would need to shift to them. My plea for help was met with what seemed like a resonating silence. Although everyone commiserated with me, each conveyed that they were too busy with their own responsibilities to help. I felt I had no choice but to retire. At the end of the semester, my twenty-five years at the university were commemorated as a brief verbal footnote during a luncheon honoring a new program coordinator.

For years, the anger I felt toward my former colleagues—people whom I had recruited and others whose jobs I had saved—involuntarily surfaced. The feelings were easily triggered. Hearing someone's name, thinking about the luncheon, even talking about some unrelated thing at the university would allow the anger to bubble through. There is an old saying that you can throw hot coals at your enemies, but you'll burn your hands doing it. My hands were scalded. As I thought about the effects of Ned forgiving his son, I remembered how much energy I spent reliving my anger and disappointment with my program colleagues. They should have acted differently. They should have answered my plea for help. They should have acted as if they were me. But they weren't.

I thought back even farther, to the time years earlier that I had received a valuable lesson on accepting capabilities and limitations, at a Buddhist retreat in northern California. At the orientation session, the abbot of the monastery reminded us that counseling was available. One reason I was at the retreat was that I was having difficulties effectively parenting my children.

"I know many of you have specific problems," said the abbot. "Since they may be of a personal nature, you may schedule time with Reverend Master Asoka."

He gestured to his right, and I saw the Reverend Master was probably in his early twenties. How could I possibly discuss my family problems with someone who only recently began shaving? Maybe this wasn't such a great idea. But I decided to stay. My appointment time was on the second day. My resistance by then had been lowered, and I was at least willing to present my problems to someone who was half my age and probably knew as much about family life as I did about the cloistered solitude of a monk. He compassionately listened as I discussed many of the poor decisions I had made and their effects on my family. Instead of jumping in when I paused between thoughts, like a good therapist he patiently waited for me to continue. For almost thirty minutes, I unloaded my burden, rattling off a litany of transgressions I regretted. Finally he spoke.

"Stan, people do the best they're capable of doing, given the circumstances of their life." He rose and left the room, leaving me to think about his response. I sat there for twenty minutes until I understood this simple yet poignant thought. He was right. Given the turbulence surrounding me, there was no reason to feel guilty because I didn't do other things. What I did was what I was capable of doing, given the circumstances of my life. Ned, I'm sure, had done his best, too. And likewise, my colleagues did the best they could, given the circumstances of their lives. I've finally forgiven them—almost.

9

Epiphany

> The clearest way into the Universe is through a forest wilderness.
>
> —John Muir

I WONDERED only briefly, at first, why Wendy didn't answer the phone. I had just arrived back in San Francisco from delivering a series of lectures on the East Coast. I thought maybe she had forgotten to turn on her cell phone. I retrieved my luggage and went outside the terminal to wait. After thirty minutes I called again. Then again after another thirty minutes. By now, I was getting worried. We lived only fifteen minutes from the airport, and although Wendy had never been good about time, this was well beyond being late. After two hours, she finally pulled up to the curb. I had just spent seven hours on a crowded airplane and I was about to take out my annoyance for having to wait for two hours. Then I saw she was crying. I left the luggage where it was and came to her side.

"It's Tom, he has a brain tumor." Tom is Wendy's older brother. "I'm sorry I couldn't answer the phone. He called just as I was leaving, and I've been speaking to him the entire time."

As we drove home, Wendy told me that Tom had developed a weakness on his left side. He would be having tests the following day. Tom, according to Wendy, was nervous but hopeful. It was a difficult night for both of us. We received a call from Tom the next day. The tumor was the size of a golf ball. But it was operable, and there was a possibility it was benign. Surgery was scheduled for two weeks later. Anything beyond that and the tumor would start pressing against parts of the brain that controlled vital organs. Tom asked if it was possible for Wendy to be there. She assured him we all would come.

The day of the operation Wendy, Jessica, Justin, and I sat with Tom in his room. After five minutes of stilted conversation, Tom said, "Wendy, I need to talk to you alone. Everyone else needs to go away."

Tom had never been good with social graces, but he never was abrupt, either. He often reminded me of a child who only learns how to be courteous after he makes a gigantic mistake. Tom's behavior toward my children was especially unusual on this day of the operation, since he had always been the doting uncle. As the three of us left, I could tell his tone and words had upset Jessica and Justin and that they both felt rejected.

"You need to understand," I said when we sat down in the waiting room, "the tumor is probably more responsible for what Tom is saying than what he's feeling." I knew the location of the tumor was already affecting his language and processing abilities. We sat silently until Wendy came out of the Tom's room twenty minutes later, crying. Regardless of the prognosis, Tom would be in the hospital for at least three days for recovery. Wendy and Jessica would stay for however long it was necessary. Justin and I would return to San Francisco in three days.

Throughout the five hours of surgery, a nurse came back and forth into the waiting room and continually assured us that it was going well. Eventually the surgeon came out.

"He's doing well. I was able to remove the tumor," he began.

I saw Wendy, Jessica, and Justin physically relax as if they were being told everything was all right. But I had a feeling there was more information coming.

"We can't tell about the type of cancer until the lab results come back."

"But you got out all of the tumor?" Wendy said in a pleading voice.

"No, the tentacles were too deep." He waited for Wendy to ask another question, but she didn't. It seemed he was more comfortable responding to questions than offering up information. When Wendy didn't say anything, I said, "They'll continue to grow, won't they?"

He nodded his head.

"And then?" Wendy asked.

"As soon as he has recovered from the operation, we'll start radiation therapy to delay it."

I could see Wendy, Jessica, and Justin beginning to look more calm. In their minds, there was a hope for a cure. Their reactions were no different from those of family members of some of the hospice patients I had known, who couldn't accept that their loved one was dying. The surgeon started talking about different treatment protocols, how long they would last, and the side effects. It seemed he was avoiding saying anything that was related to the length of time Tom had left. As the discussion with the surgeon unfolded, my family shifted the emphasis away from the serious nature of the illness toward strategies for helping Tom's recovery. Jessica and Wendy would return with Tom to Fort Lauderdale and stay to help as he got back on his feet. Justin would go to Florida to spell them if necessary, so Tom would always have someone there with him. The three of them looked at me as if they were waiting for me to give them my travel schedule. Instead, I turned my attention to the surgeon, who appeared ready to leave.

"How much time does Tom have left?" I asked. I could see by my family's reactions that this wasn't something they wanted to think about. Now all of us were looking at the surgeon.

"It's hard to say without first getting the lab results."

"I know the lab results will be more definitive, but based on your experience what do you think, now."

"I'm not really comfortable giving a diagnosis without the results." I thought he was being disingenuous. This was a world-class neurosurgeon who had done thousands of similar operations.

"Yes, I understand how important data is. But based on your years of experience, surely you must have an idea about the type of cancer it is."

He took a deep breath and said, "If I'm right, it's a glioblastoma."

I knew about glioblastomas. I had seen the effects of this

cancer in at least five hospice patients. It's the most aggressive form of brain cancer and is nearly always fatal.

"If you're right about your diagnosis, how much time does he have?"

"That's hard to say."

"Okay, then, what about a range?"

"Three to eighteen months." When he saw the look on the faces of Wendy, Jessica, and Justin, he began equivocating. "But that's variable. I've had patients live much longer. There's just no telling."

"But what you're saying," I interrupted, "is based on what you saw and believe, the prognosis is terminal."

There was a long pause, then he nodded his head and softy said, "Yes, I'm sorry, but it is terminal."

His professional demeanor changed when Wendy, Jessica, and Justin began crying. "We still can't be sure until the lab results come back," he said. "Let's be hopeful."

"But you're pretty sure about your initial diagnosis?" I said.

"Yes."

"Assuming that the lab results confirm your suspicions," I said, "who should tell Tom that it's terminal?"

"Nobody."

"Why not?"

"I've found that patients who don't know what the diagnosis is tend to live longer. We don't want to take away Tom's hope for recovery."

I looked at Wendy, who was nodding her head in agreement. I was familiar with physicians outside of hospice who looked at death as the enemy. As something that should be held at bay no matter what the physical and psychological cost to the patient. I feared this well-meaning surgeon fit into that category. When he left, Wendy was emphatic—I wasn't to tell Tom he was dying. I always respected the wishes of my patient's family members, even when I thought a mistake was being made. If I did that with strangers, I needed to do it with my own family, despite what I feared would be problems in the future.

Although I had been volunteering at various hospices for a number of years at the time of Tom's surgery, I rarely talked about my experience to my family, and then only if they pressed me. And on those rare occasions, I didn't share any of the details. So when my son and I were alone in our hotel room later that day, I was surprised when he said, "Tell me about dying. I want to know what Tom will go through." For an hour we talked. He wanted to know what my experiences had been and how I reacted when someone I cared about died. It was probably the most revealing discussion I ever had with Justin. Not because I had ever really hidden things from him. We had always been very honest with each other, even to the point of me telling him about my wilder days in college and how I felt when Wendy and I were separated for a year. But this had a different feel to it. We left the room and returned to the hospital, closer than I think we had ever been.

By the next day Tom was feeling better. He was the "old Tom," joking with Justin and Jessica and kidding with the nurses. By mid-morning the surgeon was back, examining Tom and being very upbeat with him. While Jessica and Justin remained with Tom, Wendy and I went outside the room with the surgeon.

"It's a glioblastoma," the surgeon said to us. "With the tumor removed, the pressure on his brain was reduced. And when the swelling from the surgery goes down, he'll have more sensitivity in his hand and his mobility will improve."

"How long will it last?" I asked.

"I don't know. That depends upon how effective the radiation is."

"Weeks? Months?"

"Most likely months."

"And then?"

"The same symptoms will occur along with new ones."

"Like what?" Wendy asked.

"Based on where I think it will regrow, I think you'll start seeing changes in his cognition."

"What areas?" I asked.

"It's hard to tell. But I think there will be problems in his judgment. Maybe even emotional labiality. And even some paranoia."

I had seen all of these problems in hospice patients. For some who were cognizant of what was happening, there also was depression. For those who didn't realize what was occurring, there was fear. For families not prepared for the changes, there was confusion and sometimes even anger. I feared all of these problems would occur with Tom. That night the four of us went out for dinner. As we sat in a quiet restaurant I felt it was time to explain to my family what to expect. I described the progression of symptoms and behaviors I had seen in hospice patients. They listened quietly, and I could see the tears forming in everyone's eyes as I described the changes they would probably see in Tom.

"Wendy, I know both you and the surgeon disagree with me," I said, "but I think Tom should know he's dying."

"Why not give him some hope?"

"Tom has a short amount of time to get his life in order, to make amends, to finish up business. I'm afraid that by not giving him the opportunity to do it now, by the time it becomes obvious to him that he isn't getting better, it will be too late."

"I can't tell him he's dying," Wendy said.

"I'll do it."

"No, not yet, not when he's still so hopeful."

"How will we know he's dying?" Jessica asked.

I described "active dying" to them and the types of behaviors that precede it. And finally, the actual moment of death. Suddenly, everything made sense to me, what my hospice journey was really about. It seemed to have been a path that prepared me for helping Tom die and my family to cope. It was such a profound realization I stopped talking in midsentence.

"Daddy, are you all right?" Jessica asked.

"Yes, I'm fine. I just lost my train of thought for a minute."

Justin and I flew home the next day, and Wendy and Jessica took Tom to a friend's house where he would recover for one week until he was able to fly back to his home in Fort Lauderdale. When they took him back, they stayed with him for an additional week. By then, Tom's mobility had improved and he was acting as if he was over the brain cancer. He insisted he didn't need any of us to stay with him. Wendy and Jessica came home, and we began a twelve-month ordeal of worrying about Tom and doing what little we could for him from across the country. Over and over again, we asked him to move out with us, especially as he became weaker and home health workers were hired to take care of him twenty-four hours a day.

"No, I'm doing fine here," he would repeatedly say. "Maybe if things get worse, I'll reconsider." Things were getting worse, but Tom either couldn't see it or wouldn't accept it. Within a few months, the tumor had regrown and the surgeon told him there was nothing else that could be done. As he grew weaker and more delusional, he began calling us five, sometimes ten, times a day. That's when the four of us began to take turns staying with him. One of us would stay for a few weeks until someone else arrived. There was never more than one week without one of us staying with him. Although he was having round-the-clock care, emotionally he needed one of us there as much as possible. Every time we asked him to come to California, however, he would say, "Not yet." Eventually there came a point in the progression of his illness when he finally asked to come and live with us, but by then it was too late. There was no way he could fly across the country, nor could I have driven him.

When I was in Florida, my talks with Tom now focused on his need for closure on a host of issues, closure that might make the remainder of his life less difficult. There wasn't anything that was out of the ordinary: unresolved relationships, unfulfilled dreams, and regrets. Between hallucinations we would talk about them. During hallucinations I would try to get him to focus on his surroundings, much in the same way I did with Joyce. If Tom had known earlier that he was dying, would the process have been any easier? I don't know. I knew for some of the issues, there never could be a resolution, no matter how much time he had to deal with them.

Two days after returning to San Francisco from Florida, I received a phone call from one of Tom's caretakers. She thought Tom was close to actively dying. After listening to his breathing, I agreed, and I passed this information on to Wendy.

Although Wendy had scheduled a trip to Fort Lauderdale for the following week, now she and Jessica left for Florida on the next available flight, to make sure there would be time to say goodbye to Tom. Tom sounded like he was close to actively dying, but I thought I would have at least one day before it would be necessary for me to fulfill my promise to him—to be at his side and help him die. When Wendy and Jessica called me the next morning and described Tom's symptoms, I left that evening with Justin. There were no direct flights, and we would have an hour stopover in Dallas. As soon as the plane landed, I turned on my cell phone. There was a message from Jessica.

"Daddy, please call. Tom may be dying right now and we don't know what to do."

The quietest place I could find was on the floor of a corridor connecting the terminal in which we landed and the one we needed to get to for the connecting flight. Jessica answered the phone immediately, but I couldn't understand what she was saying.

"Jessie, you have to stop crying. I can't understand you."

"I think he's dying, Daddy."

"Tell me why you think that."

"It's his breathing. It's very rapid and shallow and he's not responding to what Mom or I are saying."

"Where are you?"

"In the living room."

"I want you to go back into the bedroom and place the phone by Tom's ear so he can hear me and I can hear his breathing. Try to listen also, because I need to talk to you when I'm done talking to Tom." When Jessie held the phone to Tom, I could hear that his breathing was very rapid, shallow, and there was a gurgling sound with each breath—something's that called a "death rattle," which appears very close to someone's death.

"Tom, I know you can hear me," I said. "I promised to help you die, but Justin and I are in Dallas. We won't be in Fort Lauderdale for at least an hour. I know how frightening this is for you. Jessica and Wendy will be there to help you. We love you, Tom, and if you can wait we'll be at your side. If you can't, just let go."

"Jessica?" I said.

"I'm right here."

"Do you think Tom heard me?"

"I think so. He started to cry when you finished talking."

"There's nothing to be afraid of. Justin and I may not make it in time, but you can do some things to help Tom."

"I don't know what to do!" she said as she cried.

"Keep the room quiet, no phones or loud talking. I know it may be hard, but it's important that you and Mom remain calm. The more peaceful you are, the more peaceful Tom will become. As he's getting closer, there will be more and longer silent periods between his inhalation and exhalation. You'll also hear more of the gurgling sounds you hear now. Both you and Mom should sit down next to him and gently hold his hands. If it appears that he is becoming agitated, let his hands go. When you get off the phone, start telling him how important he has been in your life. Mom should do the same thing. She also could talk about the wonderful things they experienced growing up together. Keep it positive. That's most important."

"Is there anything else?"

"No, just remember that Tom most likely can hear you and Mom, almost to the time of his death. He may be having visions now that either are confusing or frightening. Keep assuring him that everything will be fine, that you're there with him."

"I don't know if I can do it."

"You can, Jess. Trust me, you can do it."

As soon as the plane landed, I called Jess. She had done everything I said and Tom was still alive, but it appeared that the gaps between his inhaling and exhaling were increasing.

"Tell him we're here and we'll be there in twenty minutes."

Justin and I ran through the terminal, not bothering to gather up our luggage. I found a taxicab as soon as we exited the terminal and gave the driver $20 as a tip in advance. All he had to do was get us to the apartment in twenty minutes. We were there in fifteen. When we entered the apartment, Tom's breathing was shallow and his fingertips had a tinge of blue.

"I'm here, Tom," I said and kissed him on the forehead.

Both Jessica and Wendy were very calm. "See, Jess, I knew you could do it."

Tom's favorite caretaker had arrived, and together we all talked about Tom and included him in the conversation as if he could open his mouth at any time and comment. I did some chanting and offered prayers for his journey. About an hour after I arrived, there was a dramatic difference in Tom's breathing.

"It's happening, Wendy," I said. She got in bed with Tom and held him; the four of us were touching his body as he took his last breath. We bathed Tom and dressed him in his favorite clothes; a T-shirt from a camp he attended when he was a child and the shorts he always wore to the racetrack. We stood around him and reminisced about his life. It was only then that I realized I was wrong in thinking the goal of my journey was to prepare Tom and my family for Tom's death. That was an offshoot. The purpose of the journey had always been to prepare my family for my own death.

Epilogue

Can you walk on water?
You have done no better than a straw.
Can you fly in the air?
You have done no better than a blue-
bottle.
Conquer your heart;
Then you may become somebody.

—Abdullah Ansari of Herat

It's been five years since the diagnosis, and obviously I'm still alive. Unlike breast cancer, there's nothing significant about the five-year mark for prostate cancer if the cells left the gland, which they did in my case. My hormone treatments will never kill the runaway cells, just keep them in a state of semistarvation. And just like a person deprived of food, these unwelcome guests will try to find a way of outwitting their tormentors. The ending to my story will be predictable, but the reverse of the "living happily ever after" plot. In my case, it's the bad guys who will win, unless something else kills me first.

I've been asked by some of my hospice patients if I'm afraid of dying. Some ask because they're wondering, since I've been with so many people who have died, if I may have experienced something during those deaths that gave me insight. Still others ask because they're afraid of their own death and desperately want reassurances. I always start by describing what I've witnessed at someone's death. Events that are so spiritual—words haven't yet been invented to adequately describe them. When I finish explaining what I've seen and felt, most patients become more peaceful. But some—many of those whom I have been closest to—aren't satisfied.

"Now tell me what you believe. Are you afraid of dying?" Every time I'm asked, I take a few moments to think about it—to see if my thoughts have changed.

"I don't think so, but I'm not sure," I would say. "But what's more important is that you and others have taught me how to live."

Even though I have often been present at the moment of death, and though I have helped more than two hundred people on that path, the experience of death for me is still theoretical. My spiritual beliefs do tip the balance toward the "I'm not afraid" side, but not enough to stop the scientist in me from thinking, "I can't know until I'm there." Fortunately, this existential question is not something I dwell on. I know the cancer will shorten my life. But I've come to realize that shorter and more meaningful is better than longer and delusional.

And these last five years have been meaningful. Meaningful far beyond anything I could have imagined. Not because I'm thankful I'm still alive while people I cared for died. No.

Meaningful because I've been fortunate enough to have been invited into the lives of people who taught me how to live. My cancer acted as a powerful paint remover that peeled back layers of a building's history, revealing an architectural wonder in need of restoration. My friends in hospice were the contractors.

I've felt more alive since receiving the diagnosis than in any period of my life. Don't get me wrong, "feeling alive" doesn't equate with happiness or some new-age state of bliss. Feeling alive means the barriers I've used to soften my world have come down, or at least became more porous. As Tibetan Buddhists are fond of saying, "Lean into the sharp points of your life to get over them." I've never felt as much joy as I did knowing I was helping someone on his final journey. I never felt as much awe as when I played a tune on my flute to someone minutes away from death and realized that it was a tune I'd never heard, that originated from some unknown place. I never felt as much pain as I did not being able to alleviate the suffering of someone whose soul seemed connected to mine.

The lessons have been nothing less than transformative. Mind you, I would have preferred to learn them from a crotchety old uncle rather than from cancer or the deaths of so many people. There's nothing heroic about cancer or death: both strip away falsehoods our minds have spent a lifetime creating. Cancer sucks. Death sucks. Not because they're tragic, but because both are unsettling when lives such as mine were built on a foundation of sand. As I look back on what I've learned and wonder if there could have been other ways of acquiring the lessons, I realize there weren't. To paraphrase a centuries-old saying, "A picture of an apple is not an apple."

Prior to my cancer diagnosis and my hospice experiences, I read countless books on life, attended numerous personal insight retreats, lectured on the acceptance of what can't be changed, and even gave workshops on most of the areas covered in this book. But writing, lecturing, and even listening to enlightened teachers dealing with life is not the same as living. As a university professor for thirty years, I was steeped in the world of ideas. There is beauty in the purity of thought. Ideas can be manipulated, rearranged, and given a gloss, which makes them sound appealing, even erudite. Writing about death is not the same as facilitating it. Facilitating it is not the same as dying. A picture of an apple is not an apple.

There is nothing altruistic about hospice volunteering, at least not in my case. I'm not Mother Teresa, or a detached observer, or a cultist fascinated with death. Nor did I view my coming to hospice as a "calling." I was dragged into it, kicking and screaming, not knowing why I was being led there. What hospice work helped me understand is that life isn't about thinking or observing at a distance. It's about doing, even if it involves witnessing someone in unimaginable pain and knowing the only thing you can do is embrace her. The doing of living is the soil from which knowledge develops. And it's in that magical place I've been fortunate to dwell for the last five years.

On a trip to New York, I was walking with Jessica through Greenwich Village when we came upon a children's park at Sixth Avenue and Minetta Lane. Within the park was a small cinder-block building that probably housed playground equipment. The wonderful scene painted on the building's wall by children impressed me. It was a picture of the playground with colors more vibrant than were actual. I kept staring at it, comparing the imagined with the real. We resumed walking until I noticed something written in a child's hand in the corner of the wall. It was a quote from the noted educator Marian Wright Edelman. It was the author's name that caused me to stop. But it was the words that kept me there.

> Service is the rent we pay for living. It is the very purpose of life and not something you do in your spare time.

As I think about what I've gained by serving the dying, and how it gave purpose to my life and changed me, I realize I'm not paying enough rent.

Practical Suggestions

I'VE LEARNED a number of things that are helpful for the dying and those who care for them. None are difficult or require anything other than being human and transparent. Earlier in this book I cautioned against believing that theories about dying and helping can be universally applied. The same is true for these suggestions. Life and death are messy. What I've found helpful for some patients wasn't helpful for others. Although the suggestions listed here have wide applicability, it's the situation that dictates the application.

Relax. People who have not been around the dying often become nervous, wondering if they are doing the "right things." I've found the more relaxed one is, the easier it is to do things that will help the dying person. Maybe when we relax, we become more open and willing to give without wondering why we are doing something or if it's the right thing to do. Human beings have cared for our loved ones and prepared them for death for as long as we've been human—maybe even longer than that. Genetically, we know what to do. We just need to get out of the way of our ego and allow our heart rather than our mind to take over.

Be kind to yourself. Caring for a loved one is emotionally and physically draining. and you will feel many contradictory emotions. Don't feel guilty about any of them (for example, wanting the person to stay, yet also wanting their pain to end): these feelings are normal. Take breaks by walking in a park, listening to music, meditating, or anything that momentarily stops the difficult work of caregiving and grieving. Find a person or agency to provide you with the respite you'll need to "recharge your batteries."

Sit when talking. It's a common practice to stand when talking to a person who is in bed. Although unintended, it becomes a position of superiority, both physically and allegorically. But if you sit down on a chair at the same eye level, the interaction often becomes one of equals.

Reduce noise. Try to keep unnecessary noises to a minimum. As one of my patients said to me, "Dying is hard work." The more noise that is present, the harder the work. I've found that televisions—especially in nursing homes and care facilities—are used as a distraction for patients and their families. Don't assume the dying person wants to be distracted. Always ask the person if it's all right to turn on a television, radio, or CD player. Conversations should be soft, with only one person speaking at time.

Balance help with independence. The process of dying involves the continual shifting of the balance point between being helpful and providing independence. Being overly helpful may require someone to accept their imminent death before they are ready. Allowing too much independence may come across as being uncaring. The best approach is to take your lead from the person. They will let you know what is needed and what they can still do by themselves.

Creating a calming environment. Surround the person with objects, music, and smells that are peaceful and comforting, such as pictures of loved ones, favorite places, awards commemorating achievements, favorite objects, meditative music, and flowers. If possible, remove objects that relate to their illness (for example, medications, hygienic supplies, and so on).

Don't argue. I've seen loved ones occasionally arguing in the presence of the person who is dying. It always resulted in discomfort for the person. If there are reasons for disagreeing, have the discussion out of the person's visual and auditory range. It's believed that hearing remains intact when other senses have dissolved.

Celebrating life. Although a person is dying, it's a time to celebrate their life. The celebration can involve conversations about past wonderful experiences, developing a journal for friends and future generations (dictated to you, or audio- or videotaped), a visit to a favorite place, or even a goodbye party.

Interests change as one dies. Don't assume that what was of interest to the person when they were healthy is what interests them as they approach death. Relationships become more important than either activities or intellectual pursuits (for example, sports or current events). As one approaches death, life is simplified and the focus moves to the present.

Don't talk about the person as if he or she wasn't present. Dying doesn't translate into invisibility or immaturity. When discussing anything about the person in their presence, include them in the conversation.

Listen more, talk less. In our normal lives, we often seek to fill silence with conversations. I've found this to be especially true in the presence of someone who is dying. This is a time to sit quietly, wait, and listen.

Don't rely just on words to communicate. Often words aren't adequate to communicate feelings about loved ones. Also, the person may be so far in the dying process that she or he doesn't understand what you are saying. Try using something that's more immediate and less cognitive, such as touch and vocal intonation. If you play a musical instrument, ask them if you could play. Whatever you choose to do, start using that method of communicating early in the dying process, so that when the person can no longer use words or understand them, communication is still possible.

Express compassion in little ways. Since dying is such a major event for everyone that is involved with it, we often believe that compassion needs to be expressed in big ways. It doesn't. Forget about big gestures and focus on expressing your love through the simplest of things, from the placement of flowers to sitting supportively in the presence of pain.

Discussing death. Loved ones are often reluctant to talk about death with the dying. Even if the terminal status has been withheld, a dying body is continually sending undeniable messages that it's winding down. Listen nonjudgmentally to their concerns. Don't try to convince them that they will be getting better. Don't force a discussion about dying. For some people, there is an eagerness to talk about their own death. For others, it may take time before they are ready, or the time may never occur.

Completing unfinished business. Some people hold on to life, despite pain, in order to finish "their business," which can range from saying goodbye to asking for forgiveness to completing a legal document. Completion of something identified by the dying person that needs to be finished can offer comfort as they approach death.

Saying thank you. Sometimes there is a reluctance to thank the person for all they have done and for what she or he has meant to you. Often, people believe that by thanking a dying person, it confirms that she or he is dying. Their body has told them they're dying long before you will. Thank-yous, once said, can provide great comfort.

Forgiving and asking for forgiveness. Enormous discomfort can be caused if the dying person feels she or he has done something that can't be forgiven. If they don't have the opportunity to ask for it directly from the person they believe was hurt, help them write a letter or audio- or videotape their message. Conversely, asking the dying person to forgive something that you did can also be comforting.

Don't grieve excessively in the person's presence. There is a difference between grieving the eventual loss of a person's life and overly demonstrating it in their presence. Excessive emotional displays can be detrimental to a more peaceful death. Grieve, but don't allow your feeling of loss to upset the person who is dying.

Providing food and drink. It's a natural reaction to suggest or even insist that a dying person eat or drink, "to keep up their strength," despite the person's insistence that she or he isn't hungry or thirsty. As the body begins to shut down, it no longer requires nourishment. Actually, the ingestion of food or water may be painful. Accept their decision to stop eating or drinking. The body knows when it can no longer handle nourishment.

Give legitimacy to private experiences. People who are dying may encounter visions or sounds only visible or audible to them. Although some may be frightening, most are spiritual. While some may be attributable to the physical effects of the dying process, others are unexplainable. Caregivers and loved ones are often asked what they mean. Instead of trying to interpret them, it's all right to say you don't know and to ask what the dying person thinks it means. Don't insist that it's a delusion unless it's something that's disturbing (such as being locked in a jail cell), and then only after you've asked the person what they think it means.

Giving permission to die. People often hold on to life until they feel their loved ones are ready for them to depart—often despite intense pain. There are times when it's important to give a loved one permission to die. Use simple words coupled with how important she or he has been in your life.

What to do as death is imminent. The physical ending of life is spiritual. There are various ways it can be supported. Often a person's history can provide you with guidelines. For example, someone who never wanted to be touched may feel uncomfortable with someone holding their hand or body as she or he dies. Conversely, a person who always needed physical closeness may want to be held. If you remain open to the situation and know the person's history, you'll instinctively know what to do. Don't worry about doing the "right" thing.

After the moment of death. Sit and do nothing. This is a time for you to reflect on what their life and death mean to you. If there are religious rituals, begin them. If nothing was decided beforehand, this is a time for you to begin your healing. Many people have found that cleaning the person's body in preparation for removal shows great respect and is also healing for everyone who participates. Don't be afraid to invent your own ritual.

Helpful Resources

Books

DEATH, DYING, GRIEVING

Albom, Mitch. *Tuesdays with Morrie*. New York: Broadway Books, 1997.

Buchwald, Art. *Too Soon to Say Goodbye*. New York: Random House, 2006.

Chödrön, Pema. *When Things Fall Apart*. Boston: Shambhala Publications, 1997.

Halifax, Joan. *Being with Dying*. Boston: Shambhala Publications, 2008.

Levine, Stephen. *A Year to Live*. New York: Harmony/Bell Tower, 1997.

Ram Dass. *Fierce Grace*. DVD. New York: Zeitgeist Films, 2003.

Pausch, Randy, and Jeffrey Zaslow. *The Last Lecture*. New York: Hyperion, 2008.

Sogyal Rinpoche. *The Tibetan Book of Living and Dying*. San Francisco: HarperSanFrancisco, 1994.

Thich Nhat Hanh. *No Death, No Fear*. New York: Riverhead Books, 2002.

THOUGHTS ON LIVING

Blasdel, Christopher Yohumei. *The Single Tone*. Tokyo: Printed Matter Press, 2005.

Brooks, Ray. *Blowing Zen*. Novato, Calif.: New World Library, 2000.

Dalai Lama. *Ethics for the New Millennium*. New York: Penguin Putnam, 1999.

Krishnamurti. *Commentaries on Living*. Wheaton, Ill.: Theosophical Publishing House, 1958.

Patrul Rinpoche. *The Words of My Perfect Teacher*. Boston: Shambhala Publications, 1998.

Persig, Robert. *Zen and the Art of Motorcycle Maintenance*. New York: Bantam Books, 1973.

Thich Nhat Hanh. *The Heart of the Buddha's Teaching*. New York: Broadway Books, 1999.

CAREGIVING, SERVING

Callanan, Maggie, and Patricia Kelley. *Final Gifts: Understanding the Special Awareness, Needs, and Communications of the Dying*. New York: Poseidon Press, 1992.

Chödrön, Pema. *Awakening Loving-Kindness*. Boston: Shambhala Publications, 1996.

Holland, Audrey L. *Counseling in Communication Disorders*. San Diego: Plural Publishing, 2007.

Ostaseski, Frank. *Being a Compassionate Companion: Teachings, Stories, and Practical Wisdom for Those Accompanying Someone Who Is Dying*. Audio recording available from the Zen Hospice Project at www.zenhospice.org.

Ram Dass and Paul Gorman. *How Can I Help?* New York: Alfred Knopf, 2003.

MEDITATION

Kabat-Zinn, Jon. *Wherever You Go, There You Are*. New York: Hyperion, 1994.

Hospice Agencies

There are thousands of hospice facilities and agencies throughout the country. The ones I have listed here are national clearinghouses with websites that provide lists of local agencies and helpful information about hospice, caregiving, and death. If I missed any, I apologize to the agency.

Hospice Directory
www.hospicedirectory.org

Hospice Foundation of America
www.hospicefoundation.org

National Association for Home Care and Hospice
www.nahc.org

National Hospice and Palliative Care Organization
www.nhpco.org

National Institute for Jewish Hospice
www.nijh.org

Hospice Volunteering and Training

Almost all hospices have an internal training program. The sites listed here go beyond specific site training. The agencies offer in-depth training on hospice care that is applicable to all settings.

Hospice Volunteer Association
www.hospicevolunteerassociation.org

Hospice Volunteer Network
www.growthhouse.org

Hospice Volunteer Training Institute
www.healproject.org

Hospice Volunteer Training Series
www.hospicetutor.com

Metta Institute
www.mettainstitute.org

Upaya Institute
www.upaya.org

About the Author

STAN GOLDBERG, PHD, coaches individual and corporate clients in how to effect change more efficiently. He is also Professor Emeritus in Communicative Disorders at San Francisco State University. He has authored six technical books in that field.

He is also an experienced public speaker and has published articles, poems, and plays addressing end-of-life issues. His three-act play, *Choices*, won first place in the 2007 Festival of New Work at the Oxford International Institute for Documentary and Drama in Conflict Transformation.

He is one of six essayists who were asked by NPR to read their "This I Believe" essay at a public gathering in 2007. He lives with his wife in the San Francisco Bay Area. For more information about him, visit his website at www.stangoldbergwriter.com.